Eight Fearless
Irishmen

Clive Scoular

Published in 2011 by
Clive Scoular
Killyleagh
County Down

The author gratefully acknowledges the help given unstintingly by his partner, Thomas Johnston, in the preparation of the layout and design of this book. Without his help the work could never have been completed.

ISBN 978-0-9539601-8-7

For May Boyd

whose light shone for 101 years

Contents

Introduction 6

Paul Cullen 8
Inscrutable and steadfast – a powerful prelate

Douglas Hyde 30
Indomitable and intellectual – a gentle giant of a man

Erskine Childers 58
Enigmatic and conscientious – a zealous convert

The O'Rahilly 78
Assiduous and able – the brains behind the Easter Rising

Hugh Lane 96
Enterprising and eclectic – art lover and flamboyant dandy

Thomas MacDonagh 118
Aspirant poet and playwright – a reluctant revolutionary

Michael Collins 132
Passionate and patriotic – the man of the moment

Kevin O'Higgins 158
Resolute and strong – an unbending nation builder

Introduction

For years now I have been studying and researching many of the personalities of Ireland's 19th and 20th centuries. In my recent book *The Lives of Ten Influential Irishwomen*, I concentrated on a group of women whose contribution to Ireland has been immense, in my opinion, and yet few of them are remembered.

There are so many men who have also made their mark, some well known and others forgotten. I have chosen to write about eight such men who have left their unique mark on Ireland's history.

Paul Cullen was a remarkable prelate who singlehandedly brought uniformity to the Roman Catholic Church in Ireland after centuries of disharmony and indecision. Hugh Lane's brilliant life brought the pleasure and beauty of art and paintings to ordinary Irish men and women. Douglas Hyde, the son of an Anglican clergyman, breathed life into an almost moribund language and, through the Gaelic League, restored pride in the Irish race.

Michael Collins, whose name is well known throughout the island, worked incredibly hard for six short years to bring, to a large degree, independence to Ireland by his tenacity and determination. Thomas MacDonagh was a poet and hardworking teacher and will be remembered as one of the signatories to the proclamation at the time of the Easter Rising in 1916. He died a martyr.

Erskine Childers was surely an enigma. This archetypal Englishman, on his conversion to the Irish cause, moved heaven and earth to achieve his adopted country's freedom, yet paid for his endeavour with his life. Kevin O'Higgins, the man with the iron fist, had the unenviable task of keeping the infant Free State's head above water after partition thrust on his shoulders. Yet his enemies never forgave him and he died by an assassin's bullet but a few years later. Michael O'Rahilly helped found the Irish Volunteers and his ideas were the origins of the Easter Rising. Although he did not want to see Irish blood unnecessarily spilt, he bravely joined the fray and perished in the struggle.

I trust that my readers will now learn more about these characters from my vignettes and go on to discover more about the lives of these eight fearless Irishmen.

Clive Scoular
Killyleagh
January 2011

Paul Cullen

Inscrutable and steadfast – a powerful
prelate

A sheltered childhood

The years at the beginning of the nineteenth century in Ireland were full of dreadful memories of the most cruel rebellion ever to hit the country. The events of the summer months of 1798, which brought death and destruction unknown in even Ireland's chequered past, left thousands dead and many more Irish men and women displaced. The year 1803 also saw yet another rising, short and abortive it may have been, but it reopened wounds which were only starting to heal.

Life for the Cullen family living in relatively prosperous surroundings in county Kildare, although difficult especially for catholics, was more tolerable than for most of their friends and neighbours. The reason for this was that the Cullens, unusual as it might have seemed, were wealthy and owned a large farm. Hugh and Mary had ten children in a household which also held six more children from a previous marriage of Hugh's. Such a large family was not all that remarkable, but to be a well-to-do one counted as a great advantage. And there were also numerous relatives, cousins, uncles and aunts, living close at hand, many of whom went on to become priests and prelates in the church, particularly during the rest of the nineteenth century.

On 29 April 1803, just three months before the abortive uprising led by Robert Emmet in Dublin, another son was born to Hugh and Mary at their homestead near the village of Prospect in county Kildare. They called him Paul.

He was a bright and clever child who was sent to the Quaker school in the neighbouring village of Ballitore. This was a popular place of learning for the children of the area, regardless of their religious background. It had a reputation for sound teaching and an even-handed approach to all the children who attended. Throughout those years many of the Cullen clan were pupils at the school and all clearly benefitted from their time spent there. The Quakers had been influential in ensuring the safety of the Cullens and other catholic families during the 1798 rebellion. Through their good offices life was secure and any possible 'settling of scores' during the conflict were thankfully avoided. Paul remained for four years before embarking on the next stage of his education at the renowned Carlow College where he boarded for his years there. Two of his relatives taught there and these men later went on to become Irish bishops. For the scholarly Paul a clerical future surely beckoned.

Leaving Ireland as a teenager

In 1821, when he was 18, Paul left Ireland to begin his priestly profession at Propaganda College in Rome. His young uncle, James Maher, had already preceded him to the college so the young man knew what he could expect. Rome was an exciting place with its ancient and beautiful buildings and its total adherence to the worldwide catholic religion. He was surrounded by committed Christians who lived to serve the church. He was enthusiastic and totally dedicated to his vocation. At the time Pius VII was the pope who was a kindly, benevolent and learned man.

However, when Pius died in 1823, his successor as Vicar of Christ was a much more conservative and autocratic man, Leo XII. Paul Cullen greatly admired Leo whose stance in religious matters was much to his liking. Whilst Pius had been a gentle man, he was struck and impressed by the disciplinarian Leo. Pope Leo only reigned for just over five years but it was during this time that Cullen formed his ultramontanist style which was to remain with him throughout his life. Ultramontanism advocated the supreme papal authority in matters of faith and discipline. In simple parlance this code meant an unshakable and unflinching adherence to the authority of the pope. To this code Paul Cullen swore total allegiance.

From those early days Paul Cullen possessed one steadfast ambition, that of total obedience and unwavering support to his pope in Rome. But for the pope too Cullen's loyalty was a great asset. Cullen kept in close contact with his clerical relatives back in Ireland, and his knowledge of religious matters in Ireland was of advantage to the prelates in Rome. He was regularly able to report to the Curia what was going on back in his native land and, quite quickly, Paul Cullen became an unofficial ambassador and legate. When something needed done in Ireland or when there were difficulties with an already somewhat unruly Irish hierarchy, then Fr Cullen would be able to sort it out or at least give his superiors in the Holy See sufficient information for the matter to be resolved. For such a young and lowly priest, Paul Cullen soon became a favourite with the Holy Father.

In the years when Cullen was preparing for his ordination, life in Ireland during the 1820s was still being dominated by the 'Great Liberator', Daniel O'Connell. By the end of the decade, in 1829, legislation had at last been passed in the British House of Commons to enact a degree of catholic emancipation. It had been a long struggle of over quarter of a century for O'Connell and for the people of Ireland to win their fight. The pope had been kept informed of the situation in Ireland and realised the contribution that O'Connell had been making for enfranchisement to be attained for all those in Ireland who were not allowed to vote, not only catholics but also Presbyterians and other non conformists.

As Cullen approached his ordination in the late 1820s Pope Leo continued to show a great interest in his young protégé. He even attended Cullen's defence of his doctoral thesis and congratulated him on his presentation. For the young Irish priest the confidence that the pope himself had shown in him must have been humbling. Paul Cullen was eventually ordained in either 1829 or 1830 although there has always been some confusion over the actual date. Immediately afterwards he was appointed to the chairs of Greek and Oriental languages at Propaganda College. Paul Cullen had certainly made good and he was to proceed to further build on his already substantial reputation.

Sadly his great mentor Pope Leo XII died in February 1829 around the time Paul was ordained. A more liberal pope, Pius VIII, succeeded Leo but he died just 18 months later. For Paul Cullen liberal popes were not his style and he was pleased to welcome the next pope, Gregory XVI, who proved to be a man after Cullen's own heart, a strict disciplinarian and a strong advocate of ultramontanism.

The shape of life to come

After nearly a decade in Rome, Paul Cullen had been captivated by the strict discipline of the pope's authority. Triumphalism and the pope's absolute power struck a ready chord with the young Dr Cullen as he now was. The Vatican's beliefs, ideals and regulations suited him and these tenets were taken on board without reservation. He became a true zealot for the catholic faith; he saw demonic forces in protestantism and freemasonry; he adhered to ultramontanism. His life became totally focussed, yet for the rest of his life he remained almost totally friendless. The only people he was close to were one or two members of his family and a few colleagues in Rome. There were never any chatty letters home; they were always official and distant. He never talked informally about matters relating to his work in Rome; every piece of correspondence was formal. There seemed little of the common touch in Paul Cullen for he was utterly determined to bury it in favour of his driven ambition.

Paul Cullen's meteoric rise to fame in Rome did, of course, affect his family and associates back in Ireland. They tried to involve him in solving disputes, but with little success. Had Rome asked him to sort out a problem back in Ireland, then he would have done his best. But any request from Ireland to be resolved in Rome would have the opposite effect.

He was then proposed for two very influential jobs in Ireland, that of president of Maynooth College and also for the post of rector of his old alma mater, Carlow College. These were outstanding opportunities for such a young man of barely 30 years of age, yet he disdainfully rejected both of them. His contempt for such offers of appointments would lead to enormous difficulties for him when he would eventually return to Ireland. Remaining aloof and friendless initially concerned those who knew him, both in Rome but even more so in Ireland. As the years passed by, those who were to understand the real Paul Cullen turned out to be protestant zealots who were as dedicated to their cause as was Cullen to his. This seems almost inconceivable that those despised most by Cullen should be those most in tune with his detached and steely persona.

Appointment to the Irish College in Rome

Cullen had scarcely been appointed to the important chairs at Propaganda when he received yet another prestigious accolade. In 1832, and still only 29 years old, he was selected to be rector of the Irish College in Rome. The college had been formed back in the fifteenth century but had undergone considerable disruption in 1826 when Napoleon's troops had misused it. For Paul Cullen this was a post where he felt he could influence the catholic church in Ireland for the college was still popular with young Irishmen seeking ordination. Until relatively recently all catholic clergy had to be trained on the continent of Europe although in the last years of the previous century Maynooth had started to train clergy for Ireland. But there was an ongoing problem with home-grown priests. They were too gallican, meaning that the Irish church held a doctrine asserting the freedom of the Irish church from the ecclesiastical authority of the Vatican. This was always anathema to Paul Cullen and it became his life's work to convert the Irish hierarchy to follow, without question, the authority of the pope in Rome. In this endeavour he was only partially successful during his lifetime.

Upon his acceptance of the position at the Irish College, Cullen immediately set about filling it with aspirant students from Ireland. He would only accept those who were prepared to toe the ultramontanist line and he would not tolerate any backsliders. Again he was not always successful in attaining his goal. Although the college was full to bursting point by 1835, the students needed his firm hand. Many of them had experienced the liberal ways of the Irish church before they arrived in Rome and it was some time before Cullen had knocked them into shape.

In 1840 he spent time back in Ireland trying to 'tighten up' his native church. There was opposition though he did succeed in many areas and he felt that his time had been well spent. Whilst he was absent from Rome there was trouble in the college with the students and there were complaints made against the vice rector, Tobias Kirby. Although the trainee priests knew that they would require to follow Cullen's line whilst they were in Rome, nonetheless many of them remained basically just as gallican as they ever had been. Kirby became a stalwart of the college and stayed there for the rest of his long life. He took over the college when Cullen left for Ireland in 1850 but he never was as charismatic, or as disciplinarian, as Cullen had been. However, Tobias Kirby continued to be one of the few friends Cullen ever had and both men corresponded regularly with one another for all the years of Cullen's life.

The Church in Ireland up to 1850

There were two particular issues affecting the Irish catholic church in the first half of the nineteenth century. They were gallican in nature which meant that, whilst they kept Rome more or less informed of what was going on in Ireland, the hierarchy did not really like interference in their internal church affairs. More importantly, however, the Irish bishops were ignorant of both the Italian and Latin languages which, as far as the catholic church was concerned, left Ireland's hierarchy at a serious disadvantage. They needed someone appointed to translate for them and the person chosen was, hardly surprisingly, Paul Cullen. He would act as their agent and would be paid for his work. The choice of Cullen was a two-edged sword. They knew he would be competent and fastidious in his work yet, at the same time, they knew that Cullen would do all he could to convert them to ultramontanism. But they had little alternative, as there was no one else available.

The Irish clergy not only had to keep Rome satisfied as far as possible, but they also had to keep the government at home happy, especially bearing in mind the ramifications of the post 1798 rebellion period barely 50 years past. There was always the fear of legislation being enacted which would run contrary to their wishes so they were often in the horns of a dilemma. Cullen, too, realised the potentially difficult situation the church was in and was fearful of the consequences. One particular fear was possible government interference in the appointment of bishops something which, in the end, did not transpire but which was to be a cause for real concern for some years.

Back in Ireland the hierarchy was able to use Cullen's skills and he, in turn, accumulated valuable information about them himself. One problem was priestly interference in politics, something Cullen would not tolerate. And then there were the two towering figures in Ireland at that time, the archbishop of Dublin, Daniel Murray, and the archbishop of Tuam, John McHale. Murray, on the one hand, was a saintly and gentle man, a gallicanist who supported the subsidies paid by the government to the national schools. Cullen was totally opposed to these payments as he was determined to keep church and government separate. On the other hand, McHale, who was to remain archbishop for almost 50 years, was probably the greatest thorn in Cullen's side whilst he was in Rome and for all the years he spent in Ireland. Although McHale was an ultramontanist the two prelates often found themselves at loggerheads over various church matters. Cullen tried to effect a reconciliation with 'the Lion of the West', as McHale was known, by getting him to soften his stance but his appeals fell on deaf ears and, for the next 30 years, Cullen withdrew his support from Tuam. On one occasion when the pope himself was drawn into an acrimonious row, Cullen almost lost the support of the Holy Father himself.

By the mid 1840s the question of the opening of the Queen's Colleges led to rancour and spitefulness. Men like Murray supported these colleges as they saw them as a way forward for young catholics to receive further education and degrees, but they were opposed by Cullen (and McHale) who saw in the colleges the possible threat of diverting religious practice towards the state religion.

The principal problem for Cullen was that he had been out of Ireland too long and, when he arrived in 1850, he did not understand Irish nationalist sentiments nor fully understood the situation in the country.

There was a great deal of priestly agitation in Ireland. Many bishops and archbishops encouraged this whilst others were against any political involvement by the clergy. The fact that the Irish church was gallicanist meant that it was well nigh impossible to prevent such deviances. There was much to concern the people of Ireland, not least emancipation and, by 1845, the effects of the Great Irish Famine. Cullen and the authorities in Rome fully acknowledged that Ireland was at last moving forward, yet they did not appreciate their clergy involving themselves in rebellion and illegal activities. Their job was to care for their flocks and serve their bishops but too many got their priorities wrong, at least in Cullen's eyes. It seems incredible to note that, during the Famine, many catholic clergy actually returned money donated to relieve distress and others diverted such gifts to fund totally unnecessary projects. The clergy were simply failing in their pastoral duties. Could Cullen ever improve such important matters? The answer came in 1848.

Paul Cullen returns to Ireland

As Cullen struggled with the many and diverse problems with the Irish church from his office at the Vatican, a solution conveniently presented itself. It should be noted that throughout his life Cullen's health was often a matter of concern, sometimes of great concern. He was clearly overworked and the strains and stresses of holding his post in Rome and sorting out the intractable problems in Ireland led him regularly to feel unwell. He was also depressed and his doctors recommended rest. Paul Cullen did not know the word and he usually soldiered on. During his life, nonetheless, he did from time to time have to take some time off to recuperate.

During 1848 the primate, Archbishop William Crolly, died. He had never been a popular man and the catholics of Ireland anxiously waited to hear the name of his successor. They had a long wait. In the same year came another abortive rising in Ireland, the Young Irelander's rebellion. The country was, of course, still in the midst of famine and it was to lose as many as three million of its citizens to death, starvation and emigration. By the end of that year Paul Cullen himself had been nominated to the vacant see. But he was not to arrive in Armagh until May 1850 leaving Ireland without a primate for almost two years.

Catholics, and the hierarchy, saw Cullen's appointment as a wise one. He was a young enough man to be reckoned with and most awaited his arrival with a mixture of apprehension and relief. The first things Cullen tackled when he arrived were the feuding within the church and an even more immediate problem, that of proselytising Church of England clergy who had set up missions mainly in the west of Ireland and who were converting many catholics with the promise of food and education. But chiefly Paul Cullen was seen as 'the Italian monk intent on bringing Irish catholics under papal direction for the extension of authority'. Little wonder that the people were uneasy. Archbishop Murray was not so happy with Cullen's appointment but McHale of Tuam was more positive. The new primate's reception amongst the 27 bishops of the church was cool and the government at Dublin Castle, placatory at best.

The Synod of Thurles

There had not been a national synod of the Irish catholic church since the Middle Ages so the significance of this gathering at Thurles in county Tipperary in September 1850 was immense. Of the 27 members of the hierarchy, 24 attended with coadjutors filling in for the three bishops who were unable to attend on account of illness or incapacity. Much was made about the consequence of this synod. Cullen was insistent that the ceremonies and services were strictly choreographed showing his ecclesiastical colleagues what he expected of them in their attention to the liturgy. The truth is that several of the hierarchy attended with the intention of disrupting the proceedings and hoping to denigrate their new primate. But Cullen was equal to them and successfully and diplomatically kept the company from falling into schism.

He was careful not to align himself either with the gallican Murray or the seemingly ultramontanist McHale. The main topics for discussion included the support or otherwise for the Queen's Colleges to be set up in Cork, Galway and Belfast. Cullen himself was opposed to them although he allowed his colleagues to set the tone of the debate and, after lively argument, the Colleges were opposed by 14 and supported by 13. However in the years immediately following Thurles Murray and other supporters died and Cullen was instrumental in ensuring the appointment of bishops who also opposed them. The idea of a catholic university was also on the agenda although, at this time, support was lukewarm and the financial contributions very slow at coming in. Cullen was, contrary to his original expectations, pleased at how the synod had gone. He felt able to proceed in getting the people back into the churches and the bishops to stop their quarrelling.

Now he had another idea. He decided that a rural diocese like Armagh was not the place for him. He needed to be in a wealthy and urban diocese like Dublin where he could exercise much more influence and would be at the centre of attention. He therefore shrewdly manoeuvred himself into a position where he could translate himself from the Primatial See of Armagh to the Archdiocese of Dublin. Here he could wield his authority with greater power and thus was the move effected in 1852. He was no longer the primate but this worried him little. In Dublin he could make the changes so much needed in Ireland.

Archbishop of Dublin

It went without saying that many of the clergy in Dublin diocese were wary of Cullen's arrival in the capital. In fact a large number of prominent priests actively opposed him and they knew they had a fight on their hands. They had, of course, lost their standard bearer, the saintly Archbishop Murray, who had always been against Cullen's ultramontanist tendencies. They had no alternative but to accept their new ecclesiastical leader.

One of Cullen's first decisions enraged not only his clergy but also the common people. He placed Ireland under the patronage of the Blessed Virgin Mary, thus relegating St Patrick from his patronal position. Then he got into more hot water by insisting that catholics did not consort with protestants. Throughout his entire life Paul Cullen showed a fierce bigotry against those of other faiths, especially protestants. He saw them as dangerous and sinful and not to be tolerated, and this from a man who owed his early education to Quakers who had themselves saved the Cullen family from a fate worse than death at the time of the 1798 rebellion.

Why was Cullen so full of hatred for protestants? Certainly he had to counter the proselytising of protestant missionaries, not only in the west of Ireland but also in Dublin itself. They were making serious inroads in converting the catholic masses and, as archbishop, Cullen felt he had to be seen to be vehemently challenging them. And to add to his woes he had, as his counterpart as Church of Ireland archbishop of Dublin, the scholarly and formidable Richard Whately. This was hardly a marriage made in heaven; more like one constructed in hell.

Throughout his years in Dublin Cullen had a schizophrenic view about consorting with civic and government officials. He remained aloof and refused to accept invitations to Dublin Castle. But this separatist approach soon changed when it became obvious that his company was regularly sought and that, by being seen alongside the great and the good of Dublin, the position of catholics would be seen to be enhanced. Loving pomp and ceremony, the arch-triumphalist Paul Cullen decided to change tack and attend so that he could be noticed. He even enjoyed meeting with members of the Royal family when they were in town. He realised the senselessness of boycotting the government. Many of his fellow clergy saw Cullen's hobnobbing with the government almost as treacherous, but he himself wanted to improve the status and standing of catholics in a country where they constituted the majority of the population.

During the 1850s Cullen had never an easy time. He was constantly imploring his clergy to attend to the needs of their flocks and not to be engaged in politics. He saw his chief aim to turn the stubborn gallicanist Irish church into a faithful one. He soon realised that many expected him to fill the gap left by Daniel O'Connell who had died in 1847 thereby leaving a formidable vacuum. He probably expended too much energy in his struggle with his recalcitrant priests. There were even times in these years when he wondered if he had done the right thing by moving to Dublin at all. Perhaps his backwater rural archdiocese of Armagh would have given him an easier ride. But he had made his bed so he had to lie in it. He had to face his demons, the principal amongst whom continued to be his 'bête noir', McHale of Tuam.

Ireland's first cardinal

In 1866 Pope Pius IX elevated Cullen as Ireland's first ever cardinal. Catholics appreciated the honour bestowed on Ireland although newspaper reviews were mixed. As far as Paul Cullen was concerned, however, his attitude changed and he clearly understood his new found position. He would now always accept invitations from the Lord Lieutenant. He would now have the place of honour at his soirees and would even outrank the Anglican archbishop. He had abandoned his principle of never dining or being in the company of protestants. He realised that, especially on state occasions, the cardinal's position was given pride of place. He was happy to meet the Prince of Wales on a visit; he was ecstatic when he saw the Church of Ireland archbishop relegated to a place of insignificance. In his letters to his friend Tobias Kirby in Rome, Cullen gloated.

The catholic cause in Ireland was making strides and Cardinal Cullen was determined to see the church take its rightful top place in society and embarrass the Church of Ireland which was still the established church. He continued in his triumphalist way with his presence at the opening of catholic churches, schools, hospitals and institutions. When the catholic university opened in 1864, the pope's health was drunk before Queen Victoria's. Paul Cullen enjoyed seeing the protestant prelates cringe.

But the new university brought troubles of its own. Funds were hard to come by and many of the appointments proved disastrous. Cullen had appointed the convert Englishman, John Henry Newman, as the first rector. Although there was little opposition to the choice of Newman, it was soon realised that the new rector was not the right person for the job. He was rarely present and he soon resigned. In many ways Cullen had made a fatal mistake when he promoted the causes and appointments of so many converts. This showed his contempt for the quality of home-grown Irish talent. Former protestant English luminaries seemed to Cullen the best choice for senior posts but this contention proved erroneous. Then, too late of course, Cullen had great difficulty in getting rid of these Englishmen. He finally understood that his convert appointments had been wrong and his clerical opponents, like McHale, rubbed salt into the wound.

Paul Cullen and his people

Cullen may have been a priest and a prelate but he had never had any close contact with the members of his church. In Rome he had been ensconced in various fine buildings in the Eternal City and when he came to Ireland he lived in splendid episcopal palaces. He talked often enough to his clergy about caring for their flocks but he himself had no relevant experience. Consequently he was an unpopular archbishop and most of the catholics of the Dublin diocese hankered after their late, lovable and sympathetic Daniel Murray. What made the difficult situation even worse was his constant failure to delegate. He had senior vicars general who could have helped him in his endeavours but Cullen refused to give them responsibility. He even complained about the vast array of religious who lived and worked in Dublin in the multiplicity of orphanages, hospitals and convents. He thought there were too many of them and that they were a decided financial drain on the poor of the diocese. Little wonder he was unpopular.

During his tenure in Dublin the catholic church was building many fine edifices, churches, cathedrals and other religious establishments. He brought in the best artists to adorn these buildings but he forgot one thing – and that was to employ Irish men and women to undertake the work. Italian, German and French artisans were employed and it was not until the beginning of the twentieth century, and long after Cullen's death, that the able and talented Sarah Purser shamed the catholic hierarchy into bringing in local artists to beautify their new churches.

Apostolic Delegate

It must never be forgotten that the pope had sent Cullen back to Ireland not only as a prelate of the people but also as his Apostolic Delegate. This meant that, apart from overseeing his dioceses, Cullen was to be the eyes and ears of the Holy Father in Ireland. This added responsibility did not go unnoticed by his clergy and people. He set out, almost with a vengeance, to 'Cullenise' the church and to turn it into the most ultramontanist church in the catholic sphere of influence.

He had his plans worked out or so he thought. He would ensure that Kirby in Rome would send him lots of suitable priests from the Irish College. He would use his influence to regularise the church. He would make Ireland the finest example of catholic allegiance to Rome. He did have some success. Plenty of young men came to work in his diocese although some of the new recruits tended to be single-minded and not exactly loyal to their archbishop. His problems with the hierarchy were more difficult to rectify. There were always a number of the senior bishops who refused to work to achieve the same goal as Cullen. And there was McHale. In Tuam archdiocese were to be found most of the difficulties with the proselytisers and, although McHale admitted that he was struggling with the problem, he was reluctant to seek Cullen's advice and assistance.

And Cullen had an altogether different dilemma in the north. The catholic bishops like Patrick Dorrian in Down and Connor had good relations with the protestant hierarchy in Belfast for example. Dorrian appreciated the reality of life in a part of Ireland where catholics were not in the majority. Cullen, as ever, was totally unrealistic when he did all he could to encourage the northern bishops to have nothing to do with protestants. This showed, once more, Cullen's lack of understanding of what life was like in the different areas of the country. He knew nothing of the protestant traditions which were a part of what Dorrian needed to be aware of as a bishop in the north.

In his earlier years back in Ireland Cullen got himself embroiled in all sorts of disputes. Most of them surrounded clergy involvement in politics. They were involved, along with many Presbyterian ministers, in the Tenants' League which fought evictions throughout the country. He had problems with the Catholic Defence Association and its convert Englishman secretary. In all these disputes Cullen, whilst sympathising with the causes, still would not approve of clergy participation. All these problems took a definite toll on his health and well-being. He could only vent his spleen on the man he was closest to – Tobias Kirby in Rome. The amount of correspondence between the two men over the years was enormous. It was Cullen's way of making use of a sturdy sounding board. He was often ill but rarely took time off. Mostly he stuck it out in Dublin, but, in 1855, he took time off to spend eight months in Rome. He had needed the break.

Another crisis broke out in Rome in 1860. In the War of Italian Unification that year the pope seemed likely to lose control of his extensive Papal States which would leave him with just the Vatican City under his jurisdiction. The pope's difficulties spurred Paul Cullen into action. He was infuriated that the pope was being threatened and, with support from a surprising number of Irish bishops, he set about raising funds to assist the Holy Father and to raise an Irish brigade to go to Rome to fight for the pope. Major Myles O'Reilly led a 1,000-man force to assist in saving the Papal States. Their endeavour was, however, in vain and many of the Irish contingent were killed or injured not long before the pope finally surrendered in September 1860. But the whole venture had been a fiasco and Cullen, too late it would seem, acknowledged his mistake in sending the brigade at all. He gave very little detail to his people and the public at large regarding the number of casualties and what had happened to those taken prisoner of war. He vowed never again to involve himself in any military campaign no matter how worthy it seemed. He had been suitably chastened and humbled.

1869 – an eventful year

This year brought two most significant events. The first was to affect Ireland and the second the entire catholic world. An act was passed at Westminster which disestablished the Church of Ireland. Although it did seem that such a momentous act would be on the statute books in the early 1860s it failed to materialise then. Cullen was always sceptical that such an act would ever pass, until it actually did in 1869. William Gladstone had taken the opportunity for MPs to vote on the issue and it passed into law. Not only were catholics pleased with the legislation but so also were Presbyterians and everyone else who belonged to any other church in Ireland apart from the Anglican Communion.

Cullen was content although he never wanted any of the vast available funds from the coffers of the established church. There were others, of course, who coveted the enormous funds of the church. Cullen is reputed to have asked that at least one of Dublin's two Church of Ireland cathedrals as well as some others throughout the country be handed over to the catholic church. But this was never to happen.

Paul Cullen was triumphalist at the disestablishment which made him unpopular with the Church of Ireland hierarchy and other protestants. It went without saying that he showed little compassion for Irish Anglicans who were in a state of shock.

Later in that fateful year Pope Pius IX called a Vatican Council after twenty years on the papal throne. Cullen was in his element as he eagerly assisted with the preparations and hounded his hierarchy to make the necessary arrangements to attend the ceremonies in Rome. His pressure succeeded when 21 of Ireland's bishops and archbishops made the journey to be present at the event. The principal item on the agenda was the doctrine of papal infallibility which was thoroughly debated and finally agreed. A fair number of the Irish hierarchy, however, failed to give the pope their support even after Cullen himself had explained the full meaning of the doctrine to them.

Despite the fact that all his bishops had not given the pope their support, Paul Cullen's star was clearly in the ascendancy in the eyes of the Vatican officials and the pope himself. Rome was proud of Cullen's achievements especially at his commitment to ultramontanism and his success in appointing bishops who adhered to this principle. As a cardinal who had contributed much to the advance of the catholic church throughout the world, as well as in Ireland, Paul Cullen himself appeared to many to be the worthy and rightful successor to the papal throne whenever Pope Pius IX died. But this was not to be. Pope Pius died in 1878 not many months before Cullen himself and so the chances of an Irish pope quickly receded.

The ever-present trouble with his priests

Whilst Cullen was manoeuvring senior ultramontanist clergy into coadjutor positions throughout Ireland and generally succeeding, he had continuing trouble with recalcitrant priests. Most of his difficulties came from wayward clergy in Munster and, of course, in McHale's Connaught. Many of these headstrong priests faced

Cullen's inquisition and, in many cases, he was able to silence them. They continued to disobey his rescripts and had to be called to defend their position. The most infamous case was that of Fr Robert O'Keeffe of Callan in Ossory diocese. O'Keeffe fought his cardinal tooth and nail and would not bow to his demands. O'Keeffe threatened to bring Cullen before the civil court which was an excommunication matter. The case was critical – was church law of greater importance than state law? In the end Cullen was summoned to court in May 1873, the first time a senior member of the hierarchy had been exposed to the civil law in open court. This 'cause celebre' was followed with intense interest throughout Ireland and further afield and, in the trial which lasted many days, Cullen's evidence was thoroughly examined. The case went against Cullen and he was required to pay O'Keeffe's costs. Two years later, however, in February 1875, three judges declared that the decision given against Cullen was itself against the law. O'Keeffe was then forced to submit to his bishop Moran (who was a nephew of Cullen's) and died soon afterwards.

Cullen was determined to stamp out the practice of priests involving themselves in nationalist politics. Throughout his years in Ireland this was the ever-present problem for him. His reason for opposing their involvement was the obvious fact that if priests were engaged in politics, then they were ignoring the needs of their people and thus adversely affecting their vocation. Needless to say, Archbishop McHale was taking a more liberal stance on the matter and open warfare often broke out between the two prelates. As a consequence Cullen became more and more unpopular whilst McHale was seen as the idol of the clergy.

One of McHale's priests, Fr Patrick Lavelle, was yet another thorn in Cullen's flesh. Lavelle became distracted from his priestly duties over his membership of an organisation called the Brotherhood of St Patrick. The dispute became so strident that the case was referred to Rome after McHale had complained to the Vatican of

Cullen's interference. The matter may have been eventually resolved but not without further damage to the reputation of the cardinal.

The abortive Fenian rising in 1867 caused yet more trouble and angst for Cullen. He was pleased that the insurrection came to nothing and that its leaders had been arrested and convicted. They constituted, in Cullen's eyes, more difficulties for the church and he showed his anger by blaming not only the misguided leaders but also protestants. He never let a chance go by without taking a swipe at his archenemies.

When the Home Rule debate started in the early 1870s their leader, the protestant Isaac Butt, incurred Cullen's wrath and displeasure. He saw that many catholics were following the movement and he was unhappy at any possible alliances being forged between the Home Rule leadership and his people.

It will be obvious that Paul Cullen was almost totally paranoid, always seeing protestants of any shade as his chief enemies. In truth there were few occasions throughout his life that Cullen found himself, at least by choice, in the company of protestants and he took every opportunity to belittle and denigrate them. He was a totally incorrigible man with the belief that Ireland's destiny would be a country free of members of the old establishment.

The end of an era

By the mid 1870s Paul Cullen was a mere shadow of his former self. He was becoming increasingly feeble and ill yet he worked on and took no rest. However his ill health became such a matter of importance that he was persuaded to permit a coadjutor bishop to be appointed to assist him in the Dublin diocese. The cleric chosen was Edward McCabe who was, in 1877, consecrated as Cullen's auxiliary bishop.

In Rome, in February 1878, the long serving Pope Pius IX died after over 30 years on the papal throne. Paul Cullen, though not in any fit state to travel, insisted on making the tiring journey to Rome for the funeral. There he met his friend and long-standing correspondent, Tobias Kirby, little knowing that this would be the last time they would meet. On his return to Dublin, Cullen's health continued to deteriorate. On 24 October, Paul Cardinal Cullen died working up to the end. He was 75 years old and had spent 28 of these years back in Ireland as archbishop and cardinal working to return the country to his goal of. Did he succeed and what was his legacy?

The Cullen legacy

The newspaper obituaries were almost entirely scathing of the late cardinal. This did not mean that his achievements, mainly in the building of churches and church establishments were not acknowledged, for they were, but the columnists adjudged him unflinching, domineering and radically devout. He was described as a catholic and nothing but a catholic who had won respect but never affection. He had, the papers said, returned Ireland to the despotic rule of the Vatican with his unswerving devotion to his principles. There was the expected indignant response from the protestant press who hailed him 'a relentless prelate, an implacable churchman and an ungenial recluse'. In all honesty no one could have complained about this statement but, at the time of the passing of a considerable figure in Irish life for so many years, the tone seemed harsh and even callous.

There were, of course, many words of praise and appreciation from others. His supporters declared that he had brought the catholic people of Ireland back to loyally support the Holy Father in Rome and that he had done his job magnificently. But the overall impression given in the press was rather more negative than positive. He had served his church; he had lived almost as a hermit; he had remained practically friendless throughout his life; he had religiously followed the commands of his Holy Father. His life was an enigma. However, as even he himself would have admitted, he had never taken much interest in the pastoral care of his people and had spent an inordinate amount of time driving the church towards his single minded goal of ultramontanism and warring with so many of his disobedient priests. And his lifelong fight with John McHale possibly overshadowed much of his successful work. His over zealous approach to bringing the church into line may have been too vigorous for prelate, priest and people alike. But had he not arrived in Ireland when he did, the church would surely have completely lost its direction. He did leave the church in good shape and fit for the trials and tribulations of the late nineteenth and early twentieth centuries.

Many who know the story of Paul Cullen would say, with conviction, that he left Ireland as a catholic nation where pluralism was never an option.

Suggested reading

1. Bowen, Desmond, *Paul Cardinal Cullen and the Shaping of Catholicism*, Dublin, 1983.
2. O'Carroll, Ciaran, *Paul Cardinal Cullen – Portrait of a Practical Nationalist*, Dublin, 2008.

Douglas Hyde

Indomitable and intellectual – a gentle
giant of a man

His early life

The future first President of Ireland, Douglas Hyde, was born in the little county Roscommon town of Castlerea on 17 January 1860. He was the fourth child, and fourth son, of the Reverend Arthur and Mrs Bessie Hyde. Their older sons, Arthur and Oldfield were then 6 and 5 years old respectively. Sadly their third son, Hugh, died in infancy. The Hyde family was completed five years later when their only daughter, Annette, was born. For the first seven years of his life young Douglas lived at Kilmacranny, county Sligo, in the rectory where his father was the Church of Ireland clergyman. In 1867 the Hydes moved back into county Roscommon to Tibohine parish, outside Frenchpark. There the Reverend Hyde remained as rector until his death in 1905. For generations the Hydes had been Anglicans on both sides of the family. Douglas's father and paternal grandfather were Reverend Arthur Hydes and his maternal grandfather was the Venerable John Oldfield. The hope and expectation of the Reverend Arthur was that at least one of his three surviving sons would take Holy Orders. In the end he was to be disappointed.

At Frenchpark the local landlord was Baron de Freyne and, as minor gentry themselves, the Hydes enjoyed the life and style of the landed classes. Lord de Freyne's brother, John, also lived close at hand in a fine house called Ratra, close to the beautiful Lough Gara, later to become Douglas Hyde's own home.

Douglas, like his older brothers, was educated at home. His tutor-in-chief was his father who was an extremely learned, if somewhat irascible, man. But the boy's most enthusiastic teachers were his neighbours who taught Douglas his first love, the Irish language. From his earliest days he sat around the home fires learning the basics of the tongue still used by the majority of the local tenants on the de Freyne estate. Douglas not only learned to speak the language but was also soon mastering such intricacies as grammar and phonetics. He was enthralled by all he heard and, by age fifteen, he moved with ease into the role of seannache or storyteller. But two years previously, in 1873, he nearly missed the wonderful opportunities being offered to revel in his native language. His parents decided to send him to a boarding school in Kingstown (modern day Dun Laoghaire). Neither of his older brothers had been sent away from home making Douglas feel downhearted and dejected. But the experiment was short lived, much to the boy's delight. Having immediately been ostracised by his new Anglo-Irish schoolmates, Douglas took ill and was returned home. Now he could simply carry on with his life as if he had never been away.

During his teenage years, Douglas roamed the countryside amidst the bogs, rivers and lakes surrounding the Frenchpark rectory. He became a more and more proficient Irish speaker; he practised what he had learnt in a diary which he started to write (and which he continued to use for the greater part of his life from then on); he determined, at that early age, to promote the use of the language before English entirely took over and Irish declined into oblivion. This was to become his life's work. He had, of course, lots of other tasks to perform as the son of a rectory set amidst the Irish countryside. Whilst the rector did have staff working for him, the Reverend Hyde and his sons had many and varied duties to carry out. Douglas loved this work. He worked in the fields, planting and bringing in the harvest; he regularly attended the markets in the neighbouring towns of Frenchpark, Castlerea and Ballaghaderreen where he bought and sold animals; he became proficient in the use of farm tools and implements. He was an accomplished young lad and was seen as a willing worker, not only by his father but also by his neighbours, the tenants on the de Freyne estate.

Life for Douglas, filled as it was with hard work and essential learning, also had its fun and he participated in all kinds of sports. He liked boxing and would have had matches with many of his friends, sustaining many a black eye in the process. He enjoyed the so-called 'garrison' games of cricket and tennis which were played both at the rectory and at the lavish grounds at the homes of the local gentry. Douglas, whilst an enthusiast for traditional Irish ways and games, still took pleasure in scoring runs for his cricket team against the town garrison, for example, or volleying to success in a tight game of tennis with his friends and relatives. Douglas's greatest passion in the field of outdoor sport was, however, shooting. He was a deadly accurate shot and spent all of his life, from his youth to his old age, clambering over ditches and bogs, with a rifle over his shoulder, in pursuit of some innocent duck, goose or plover, or some hapless rabbit or hare. Anything that moved became a target for the indomitable young Hyde and, sadly for the benighted animal or bird, he rarely missed. The obsession and fervour for the gun never left Douglas Hyde.

Progress in life and family concerns

Life at the glebe house (the rectory) was often strained. The Reverend Hyde was a hard man to live with and the health of the family regularly caused worry. His father suffered from gout brought on largely by the over consumption of alcohol; his mother was never well as she was a chronic asthmatic; Arthur and Oldfield succumbed to all sorts of unspecified illnesses. Young Douglas himself was not immune either. He had recurrent muscle pains and, for many years, suffered from trouble with his eyelids. The family doctor was, therefore, a regular visitor and trips to Dublin by train to attend specialists were a common occurrence. The Reverend Hyde had, of course, his priestly duties to perform; the visitation of the sick in his parish; the preparation of candidates for confirmation; the selection of texts for his weekly sermons. His family, and naturally enough young Douglas, were keen worshippers at Sunday services. For many years Douglas had responsibility for the Sunday school, a job he saw as a requirement of the son of the rectory rather than a labour of love. But he always ensured that he carried out his role as teacher to the children of the parish who greatly loved their kindly tutor.

Douglas's greatest friend was Seamas Hart who taught him all kinds of stories, poetry, legend and Irish folklore. Seamas was older than Douglas but it was from him that the young scholar learnt the rudiments of the language that would fire Douglas's life from then on. Tragically Seamas died in 1875 when Douglas was just fifteen. He was devastated and Seamas was deeply mourned, not only by Douglas, but also by everyone in the community. Seamas Hart had been Douglas's Irish father and, throughout his long life, he never forgot the influence that Seamas had over him.

Now that Seamas was dead and his two elder brothers had gone off to Trinity College in Dublin, Douglas was left alone with his parents. He and his father, whose relationship could be described as barely tolerable at best and antagonistic at worst, now spent a lot of time together. After all, his father was his chief educator and the person in his life who would teach him the finer aspects of minor ascendancy lifestyles. At the same time they would have discussed the first stirrings of talk of Home Rule for Ireland and the influence that Charles Stewart Parnell was having upon the populace. It was an exciting time, rather favoured by Douglas but not so by his father. For the Reverend Hyde there was one, as yet unresolved, concern. Which of his sons would follow in the family tradition and enter Anglican Holy Orders? Arthur and Oldfield had gone off to Dublin and had declined to opportunity to study divinity. With numbers one and two sons rejecting the church, the focus fell upon Douglas, the youngest son and the last chance to redeem family honour. Douglas was even taken off by his father to see the bishop but, although Douglas was working exceedingly hard, he was as yet unsure as to which vocation to embrace.

His Irish was improving by leaps and bounds and he was speaking the language, mainly with the tenant neighbours, at every opportunity. His writing of Irish, too, was so much better. The only down side was strange to relate, however. Douglas was beginning to drink a lot of whiskey and even poteen and he was still just seventeen years old. Although this did not present too much of a problem it was something he had to be aware of.

It was in the summer of 1877 that Douglas, accompanying his mother on a visit to a Dublin doctor, first encountered a number of well-known Irish speakers. He had the good fortune to attend a meeting of the Society for the Preservation of the Irish Language and there met Thomas O'Neill Russell, a prominent member. It was Russell who sent Douglas a letter in Irish, the first such missive that the lad had ever received. Russell soon became one of Douglas's mentors and a lifelong friend.

Douglas spreads his wings

Douglas spent a few weeks in France and Switzerland in the summer of 1878. He seems to have gone on his own but from this first continental experience he grew to enjoy France particularly. On his return through London, he had the great good fortune to attend an auction of Irish books which had belonged to the great scholar, John O'Daly. He spent some days viewing the books on offer and, having a few pounds in his pocket to spend, he eagerly awaited the auction itself. Although he was not able to buy all the titles he would have liked, he did make some excellent purchases and returned to Frenchpark in high spirits. Back at home, however, his enthusiasm was soon dented when he discovered that his brother, Oldfield, who had recently returned from Trinity, was beginning to drink too much and that, in fact, he and their father were becoming alcoholics. His older brother, Arthur, was also ill and was recuperating at their aunt Frances's home at Mohill in neighbouring county Leitrim. Added to all these misfortunes and encumbrances Douglas himself was not too well either and had to be prescribed glasses to alleviate his eye problems. Douglas, at just 18, had practically taken on the role of sole family overseer and protector. Matters deteriorated and, on 14 May 1879, Arthur died of consumption aged just 26. Douglas was not even able to attend the funeral because he was in London at the time consulting a specialist about his eyes. The death of Arthur came as a terrible shock to both his parents. Having lost a son in infancy they had now watched as their firstborn succumbed to a disease which was no respecter of its victim's station in life.

On Douglas's return following the funeral of his brother, he himself fell ill with pleurisy and took weeks to recover. His father was becoming more and more of a problem at home with his excessive drinking and a temper which worsened as the days went by. His mother was ill and Oldfield had been barred from the house because of his overindulgences. It was a very gloomy time at the glebe house.

Douglas recovered and continued to work on his writing and to improve his Irish speaking. He decided to Irishise his name and thenceforward he became known as Dubhglas de h-ide. At the same time he also gave himself the pseudonym 'an craoibhin aoibhinn' which translates into English as 'the delightful little branch'. His conversion to the Irish language was, so to speak, now complete. To crown his achievements in this his twenty first year, 1880, he had his first Irish poem published and many Dublin publications were favourably reviewing the work of this new poet, Dubhglas de h-ide.

Trinity College, Dublin

In June 1880 Douglas sat his entrance examinations for Trinity. His results were nothing short of brilliant. He came 5th out of 174 candidates in Virgil and was, hardly surprisingly, first in Irish. And so he became a Trinity student. However, apart from going to Dublin to sit his examinations, he remained firmly ensconced in Frenchpark. There he studied diligently whilst still participating in his country hobbies of hunting, shooting and fishing. During his first two years as a student Douglas won many language prizes. His first love was, of course, the Irish language but he was also most proficient in others like French and German. His eyes continued to give him problems and he was able to prevail upon his father to let him live in Dublin from the end of his second year. For him joy was now unconfined. He would now be living at the heart of university life where scions of the Irish language would be ever present. And so it was. He joined a number of clubs and societies which promoted Irish including the Gaelic Union. And he had made the decision his father dreaded. Douglas Hyde would not proceed to become an Anglican clergyman. This not only saddened his father but it also enraged him and Douglas had to spend his next break at Frenchpark dealing with the violent outbursts of a disillusioned father. But he survived the outrages of his parent and returned to Trinity with its abundant opportunities.

Like so many other well-known names in Ireland's history, Douglas Hyde joined the Historical Society, the 'Hist', and here he excelled in his skills of oratory and the contributions he made to its oft times heated debates. He continued to attach himself to such clubs as the Young Ireland Society and the Contemporary Club and it was through these connections that he met W. B. Yeats and the vivacious Maud Gonne. They in turn it has to be said were delighted and honoured to make Hyde's acquaintance. Between 1884 and 1888, by which time Douglas was 28 years old, he had received multiple degrees, honours and prizes. He had remained within the Divinity faculty until 1886 by which time he had been awarded BA (Honours). He then moved to Law and was gazetted LLB in 1887 and LLD in 1888. Throughout these academic years he had continued in his advocacy of a realistic approach to the Irish language and became very eminent in this field.

On 25 August 1886 Bessie Hyde died aged just 52. She had suffered numerous illnesses throughout her life yet had usually managed to recover. Life became all the more tense after Mrs Hyde's death with the Reverend Arthur regressing and being impossible to live with. For many years thereafter, right until his death in 1905, the burden of caring for their father fell firmly onto the shoulders of Douglas and his sister, Annette. One must often wonder how his faithful congregation was able to put up with Mr Hyde's vagaries and difficult behaviour and how much they would have been able to glean from his weekly sermons.

For Douglas, sorrow and heartbreak seemed ever present amidst his academic successes. During the summer of 1887 he had spent more time in France. On this occasion he had been accompanied by his great Trinity friend, Mackey Wilson. By the end of the year Mackey was dead leaving Douglas disconsolate. Throughout his life Douglas had so many friends and mentors to grieve over, not only Mackey but also Seamas Hart and members of his own close family.

Douglas's friendship with W. B. Yeats grew over the years from the mid 1880s. Whilst they regularly worked on projects together and liked one another, Douglas felt that Yeats was a social climber and what he called a 'blather'. True to form Yeats used Douglas whenever he needed something done. Yeats liked to be widely known and talked about whilst Douglas Hyde preferred to remain more anonymous, especially when it came to writing and publishing his poetry under a pseudonym. This Yeats could never understand. In 1889 Douglas had his first book on storytelling published in Irish, of course. It was quite a success although very few people knew the true identity of the author.

Douglas, now 29 years old, was beginning to wonder if he would ever land a position as a professor, something he truly wished to attain as soon as possible. He did not want to remain a perpetual student. Then a most unlikely offer was made to Douglas Hyde. An acquaintance of his, Willie Stockley, was a professor at the University of New Brunswick in Canada and he was taking a year's sabbatical. A replacement was required and Douglas was appointed to the post for the academic year, 1890-1891. He gladly accepted and made preparations to travel across the Atlantic.

His Canadian interlude

Douglas realised that he was heading off to north America to undertake his first professional job. He was elated and looked forward to the challenges there, confident that he would easily master them. He bade farewell to his father and to Annette who was now left with the sole responsibility of caring for their cantankerous parent. Douglas did suffer some pangs of guilt but knew he had to take his opportunity. He sailed from Liverpool for Fredericton, New Brunswick, on 11 September 1891. The voyage was, of course, a unique experience for him and he certainly enjoyed it. He met interesting people and seemed to relish a journey which proved quite a stormy one. On arrival in Canada on 22 September he introduced himself to the staff and students at the university. He was anxious to get on with his teaching. He took classes in French, German and English literature principally but was somewhat disappointed when he discovered that most of his students were not very bright. Nonetheless he persevered and became a popular professor.

In his spare time during the cold Canadian winter Douglas took every opportunity to go hunting and fishing, activities which reminded him of home, although he had to admit that Roscommon was not quite as cold as New Brunswick. At all times, too, he kept up a steady correspondence with Annette to give his advices as to how best to cope with their father. He considered making a journey to Boston over the Christmas holidays but decided against this as he had been given the chance to spend time in the local wilderness. He accompanied two traders from Fredericton and three Milicete Indians on what was to be a most exciting trip. They did shoot birds and catch fish but, much to his chagrin, they never bagged a caribou. It had been a memorable experience but the part he remembered best was his contacts and conversations with the native Indians. He found them charming and also discovered that their language resembled Irish in many ways. By the end of the journey he had picked up the rudiments of yet another native tongue which greatly pleased him.

Back at the university he continued his classes and spent a lot of time with his colleagues and their friends. During this time he fell in love with a number of the pretty young women whom he met and had a close relationship with a girl he always called 'the fraulein'. Her name was known only to Douglas and, when quizzed about his special girlfriend, Douglas remained the true gentleman and didn't say a word. At the conclusion of his nine-month stay at the end of term, the students and professors made a presentation to Douglas who had certainly made a wonderful impression on all of them. Before finally leaving north America he spent time in Boston.

In Boston Douglas became quite a personality and was fêted and lauded by all kinds of Irish American groups. He even had the chance to meet and interview the veteran Fenian, Jeremiah O'Donovan Rossa, an encounter he cherished throughout his life. He made many speeches during this short visit. He encouraged Irish Americans to keep supporting the survival of Ireland's native language. He was impressed by the enthusiasm of the Americans and was flattered that they had read his books and publications. His name, he discovered, was well known in that city. His parting shot to these good people was to help promote and improve the Irish language and Ireland's literature and poetry. He sailed for home full of confidence and ready to carry on his campaigns. He arrived in the port of Londonderry on 25 June 1891 which turned out to be the very day that Charles Stewart Parnell married Katherine O'Shea. Douglas Hyde had returned to his native land at a most auspicious time. There was work to be done.

Return to Ireland and time in London

On his arrival back in Frenchpark, Douglas quickly fitted into the social routine of country life in county Roscommon. There were dances to attend, cricket and tennis matches to be played and many other activities which he thoroughly enjoyed. But there was a nagging doubt in his mind. Would he now be successful in obtaining a university post? Having his credentials greatly enhanced following his term in Fredericton, Douglas hoped that he would soon be gainfully employed. He applied for posts in Belfast and even in Chicago but, after months of waiting, nothing came of his applications. He soon realised, or so he thought, the reasons for the deafening silence from these prestigious seats of learning. His enthusiastic promotion not only of Irish literature, but also of the

Irish language, had surely gone against him. There were still too many of the stuffy ascendancy professors like J.P. Mahaffy at Trinity who were determined to prevent Douglas Hyde from ever being appointed. For some considerable time they succeeded in leaving him without an appointment. He was now 31 years old. The gloom and despondency which prevailed in his own life at this time was further accented by the death, on 6 October 1891, of C.S. Parnell. The news devastated Douglas along with many thousands of Irish people. It was time to change tack and he headed for London early in 1892.

The name of Douglas Hyde was becoming very well known in the English capital. As soon as he arrived he was invited to join the Irish Literary Society and given work to do on their behalf. He was pleased at this recognition of his writing and it was not long before Dublin started a branch of this society which they simply called the National Literary Society. Douglas was then invited to become its first president, an honour he graciously accepted. On 25 November 1892, he made probably the best-remembered speech of his entire career. As president he spoke 'On the Necessity of de-Anglicising the Irish People' and in this unforgettable discourse he encouraged all Irish people, nationalist and unionist alike, to adhere to what he described as the reasonable principles which he had expounded. Ireland, in life and language, should be its own country and not simply an appendage of Great Britain. The message was well received in many quarters but not, unsurprisingly, in others. But Douglas Hyde was now, without doubt, a favoured celebrity within aspiring Irish language circles.

Marriage and the founding of the Gaelic League

In May 1893 Douglas became engaged to Lucy Cometina Kurtz. She was a friend of his sister and they had not been acquainted very long before they were betrothed. Lucy was an intelligent and well-read young woman, an ideal partner for Douglas. They married in London on 10 October 1893 and spent a lengthy honeymoon in

Douglas's beloved France. To add to his pleasure at being married he soon heard that he and his wife would be living in a house he knew well from his childhood, the beautiful mansion called Ratra which had been owned by a brother of Lord de Freyne, John French. From the early days, however, it should be noted that Lucy did not much care for either Ratra or the rolling countryside of county Roscommon. She had always been used to city life and to be thrust into such a rural community would cause her some anxiety. The young couple's return to Frenchpark was ecstatic. The locals gave them a rapturous welcome and soon became acquainted with Mr Douglas's new wife, whom they took to immediately.

1893 was to be an annus mirabilis for Douglas Hyde. Not only had he married his beloved Lucy but also he now found himself at the head of an organisation, which immediately confirmed him as president, the Gaelic League. He had long been aspiring to set up such an organisation to ensure the retention of Irish speaking in the Gaeltacht areas in the west of Ireland. Here spoken Irish was on the decline and he now determined to reverse this trend. He made great progress in this endeavour.

Over the next few years Douglas spent innumerable hours visiting and speaking to new branches of the League throughout the country. The increase in the numbers coming forward to teach Irish was nothing short of spectacular. His greatest friend was Fr Eugene McGrowney who became a great inspiration to Douglas. They worked hard together and made excellent progress. But soon McGrowney fell ill and was sent to America to try to recover his health. Sadly, however, he died of TB in 1899. The Gaelic League had lost one of its finest enthusiasts. Douglas mourned his passing and always cherished Eugene's memory.

In 1894 and 1896 Douglas's and Lucy's two daughters, Nuala and Una, were born, much to their parents' joy. But, like so much in the Douglas Hyde story, happiness was mingled with sadness. The year after Una was born, Douglas's brother, Oldfield, died. He had led an unfulfilled life as a policeman having, in earlier life, excelled in his university studies. The original Hyde clan of four sons and a daughter was now reduced to just Douglas and Annette and their irascible father who still needed constant care.

Now well established at Ratra with his Gaelic League duties, Douglas started to consider whether any university might offer him a professorship. He realised, of course, that his fervour for the Irish language and his nationalist tendencies would stand in his way amongst the staid and sober grandees at Trinity and elsewhere. He had plenty of excellent references but his attempts to find a job seemed thwarted. It was only now that he began to realise that his wife was unhappy living in the home he so greatly loved.

Meanwhile the League prospered with thousands of people enthusiastically embracing Irish. There were of course members whose keenness wore off but for so many others the chances given to them were much appreciated. Douglas continued to collate stories and poems and had the pleasure to become friendly with The Raftery, the blind Connaught poet. And he became more acquainted with Lady Augusta Gregory of Coole Park near Gort in county Galway. This friendship was also to be long lasting and Douglas's first task was to teach Irish to Lady Gregory. He had been working on his book *Literary History of Ireland* for around twenty years and, at long last, it was published in 1898. It became an instant success amongst devotees of the language and received most favourable reviews in the world's press. His struggle with Mahaffy at Trinity and his advocacy of ensuring the teaching of Irish eventually proved successful for Douglas. Mahaffy had declared that there was no sense in teaching a dead language to students at school and university. Douglas's tenacity in refuting these views in front of a government commission won the day and legislation was passed to give Douglas and his followers victory in promoting Irish in all educational establishments. During the first years of the twentieth century those presenting themselves for Irish examinations trebled in number. The Gaelic League had notched up a real success.

The renaissance of the Irish theatre

By the end of the 1890s Lady Gregory, Willie Yeats and John Synge had been translating their ideas for an Irish theatre into reality. They were enthusiastic about the project and were keen to involve Douglas. They rightly considered that their Irish Literary Theatre should present plays and works in the Irish language and Lady Gregory did all she could to encourage Douglas to write a play in Irish. He saw that the concept was one to be supported and he watched with interest how the public was reacting to the new theatre and its productions. It was generally acclaimed although the works being performed did have their detractors as well. This was only to be expected and Lady Gregory thought that she could silence her critics by having an Irish play, written by an Irish language enthusiast like Douglas Hyde, acted on stage. Douglas was sympathetic but explained to Lady Gregory that he was inundated with Gaelic League work. This was certainly not just a subterfuge. New branches were springing up all over the country and Douglas was expected to address as many of these groups as possible. By 1899 there were well over 100 Gaelic League clubs, which pleased him enormously, but he did already suspect that there were some factional differences appearing amongst some of the more established branches. He had to deal with any problems that arose and set about smoothing the fraying edges.

At home too Lucy had become chronically ill with countless unspecified complaints. Douglas, of course, was most concerned for his wife's well-being and even called on his Dublin doctor friend, George Sigerson, to attend her. He prescribed all sorts of pills and potions but Lucy never seemed to improve. Deep down she did not like living at Ratra amidst what she considered the wilds of Roscommon and this may well have exacerbated her illnesses.

At length, however, Augusta Gregory's tenacity prevailed. During a visit to Coole in the company of Lucy, Douglas relented and, with Willie Yeats to assist, a play in Irish was written. *The Twisting of the Rope*, his first theatre comedy in Irish, brought Douglas instant fame. It was played in the Gaiety Theatre in Dublin in October 1901 and became a favourite for many years to come. Douglas even acted in the play himself, which heaped much additional praise upon his shoulders. This encouraged him to write more and his obvious success meant that other budding playwrights were keen to add their contributions as well. The Irish Theatre went from strength to strength with the public clamouring to take their seats to enjoy productions written by Irish men and women and acted by local actors and actresses. As in every successful venture, however, everything did not always run smoothly. Douglas's Christmas play, which he had completed by the end of 1902, did not appear until almost a decade later because of vehement opposition from a number of Kilkenny priests. When it did eventually reach the stage in 1911, it was popularly acclaimed.

Troubles in store

From about 1903 onwards, Douglas and the Gaelic League had to contend with the increasing suspicion exerted on the League's activities by the Dublin Castle authorities. They were suspicious of the growth in public enthusiasm for the plays at the Irish Theatre. As a consequence a number of Douglas's (and others') plays were diplomatically kept off the stage to prevent further intervention and possible interference. Douglas always tried to avoid controversy for he considered that such attention would only detract from the Gaelic League's main principle of teaching the Irish language.

Further rumblings of discontent were emanating from members of the League. A campaign to demand the right to address letters and parcels in the Irish language raged on for years. The government, despite countless pleas and deputations to its officials, would not relent. Douglas even went to visit the Postmaster General, Lord Stanley, but no concessions were forthcoming. And to add to the confusion a further campaign to allow the names of cart owners to be written in Irish also reared its ugly head. A test case was taken to court by a protégé of Douglas's, the young Patrick Pearse. He lost the case (it was reputed that this was actually the only time he acted in his professional capacity as an attorney) and so this crusade on behalf of the Irish language failed miserably too.

Douglas was beginning to find life very stressful and he felt it necessary to remind his followers that he was in the forefront of de-anglicising the Irish people. He was, after all, the first person to write a book in modern Irish; the first to collect folklore in Irish; the first to collect poetry from the mouths of the Irish speakers; the first to write a play in Irish and act in it himself; the first to write a literary history of Ireland; the first to address a mass meeting in Irish and the first to persuade the Irish themselves to speak Irish to their children. His pleas had thankfully fallen on receptive ears.

The League's next problem was finance, or rather the lack of it. With money being used to employ teachers throughout the Gaeltacht areas and to send reading material throughout the land, the funds of the League were in a critical state. Douglas, like so many before and after him, appealed to his friends in America. John Quinn was a very influential man in the Irish American community and was pleased to help following Douglas's contact with him. Quinn suggested a lecture tour which was a sound idea. But Douglas was in all sorts of dilemmas. Lucy did not want to go overseas; she also wanted to leave Frenchpark because of its extreme isolation; she wanted to move to live in Dublin or even Cork. Douglas himself was in two minds. He liked the idea of undertaking a lecture tour, but he still had no job and hoped for a professorship at Cork University which was advertised at the time. He was hopeful of being appointed. So he made his excuses to Quinn citing all these difficulties, all the while realising that his thinking was muddled and incoherent. He wrote to John Quinn asking him to cancel the trip. After a few weeks, however, he realised that he was not going to land the Cork post and got in touch with Quinn pleading with him to reinstate the tour. Quinn happily obliged and, accompanied by the still reluctant Lucy, Douglas sailed for America in November 1905.

1905 had been a difficult and stressful year. He had also lost his father, the Reverend Arthur, who had died at the glebe house, having been rector, of Frenchpark, through thick and thin, for 38 years. Douglas and Annette were naturally saddened by the passing of their father, but relieved that their work of looking after him was over.

The American tour

Douglas and his wife were fêted by Gaelic League members and treated to a magnificent banquet and procession in their honour prior to their departure by train from Dublin to Cork. At Cobh (then called Queenstown) there were more receptions and cheering crowds. When the couple arrived aboard the *SS Majestic* in New York, they were greeted by John Quinn and a carefully choreographed assembly of dignitaries. Douglas quickly came to appreciate the meticulous preparations made by John Quinn who had arranged a seven-month tour throughout the United States and Canada. Although Douglas delivered many successful and inspiring lectures, he could see that, even in America, there existed much factionalism and dissension amongst the ranks of the Irish Americans.

Fund raising was the chief problem. After all, it was to collect much needed dollars that the tour had taken place. Their fundraiser, Thomas Concannon, proved inefficient and was not up to the job. Douglas was encouraged to sack Concannon, but it took some time for him to act. Money was not coming in the way they had hoped. In San Francisco the Hydes had a wonderful reception and netted a considerable haul for the League's dwindling coffers. But, even here, fortune deserted them. The horrendous San Francisco earthquake struck, with devastating effects, not long after they had left the city for the east coast. Many people were killed; large parts of the beautiful city were ruined; the once vibrant economy had collapsed. Douglas immediately sent back much of the money which had been donated to the cause to assist the struggling citizens of San Francisco in their hour of need.

Despite these difficulties the tour had been a moderate success and John Quinn had excelled himself with his outstanding arrangements. The money which had been received would do much to help with the precarious funds of the League. Douglas and Lucy left New York on 15 June 1906. Lucy, who initially had not wanted to travel with her husband, had been surprised at how much she had enjoyed her stay. She had made many friends and had experienced the high life once again. When the Hydes returned to Ireland League members were overjoyed to see their leader and president. As they passed through Cork, Kilkenny and Dublin Douglas was thrilled to receive the freedoms of these three cities. Douglas Hyde, the president and founder of the Gaelic League, had come of age. Their first stop was a joyous reunion with their daughters, Nuala and Una, who were now twelve and ten years old respectively. It was a happy meeting after seven months apart.

The situation back in Ireland
The workings of the Gaelic League continued to be fraught with difficulty as Douglas was soon to find out. There seemed a lack of enthusiasm and still many priests were not giving their unequivocal support to language classes which were, in Douglas's opinion, the central tenet to the very existence of the League.

By the start of 1907 Lucy was once again pestering Douglas to move away from Frenchpark and Ratra and to live in Dublin. By the middle of the year he had given in and some tentative preparations were made. But Douglas contracted pneumonia at the end of the year and nearly died. It took a long time for him to recover and it was not until the following January 1908 that he felt fit and well. The members of the League, relieved that their president had been returned to good health, then presented a magnificent gift to him. They had initiated a collection for Douglas and bought Ratra for him. What could he do but accept their immense generosity. Lucy was pleased for her husband yet displeased that she would now need to stay put. She would not be moving to the metropolis any time soon.

By 1908 a National University had been established and much of the pressure and fight had been led by Douglas Hyde. An act of parliament was passed and Douglas found that he had been voted on to the new senate. His first endeavour was to ensure that Irish was made a compulsory subject and, after a bitter struggle with his diehard opponents, he won the case in 1913. One of Douglas's implacable opponents was Fr Patrick Dinneen who had links with the Sinn Fein movement. He was amongst a few reactionaries who had pushed for the overthrow of Douglas Hyde as Gaelic League president. The matter went to a vote with Douglas easily overcoming the bothersome Dinneen.

At long last Douglas was appointed as the head of Modern Irish at the new university. Almost fifty years old, he had finally achieved his professorship. He was delighted also to hear that another appointee was his friend, Eoin MacNeill, who would later figure prominently in Irish history within the next few years. For Lucy came the news not only that Douglas had realised his ambition but also that they would be moving to live in Dublin, to a lovely house at 1 Earlsfort Place. She was overjoyed, and, for her husband's sake, they still kept Ratra where they would spend their holidays.

The appearance of the revolutionaries

For many years Douglas had managed to keep his Gaelic League free from those who advocated physical force. His teachers continued to travel the countryside giving instruction in Irish to thousands of eager students; his administrators still managed to spread the League's creed by post; any quarrels and disaffections had, in the main, been silenced. But the winds of change in Ireland started to blow midway through the first decade of the twentieth century and various diverse groups began flexing their muscles. Arthur Griffith had founded Sinn Fein in 1905 and members of the League, initially keen supporters, were choosing to join other organisations intent on a less constitutional approach to an independent Ireland.

Funding was becoming a perennial problem and the money raised during Douglas's 1905/6 tour of America was exhausted. After 1910 other Gaelic League aficionados were despatched to the United States in an attempt to replenish the coffers of the League. Fionan Mac Coluim and Fr Michael Flanagan toured, lectured and implored only to return with a relatively small amount of funds. Even the eccentric Roman Catholic aristocrat Sir Shane Leslie (a relative of Winston Churchill) did all he could to raise much needed funds but without much success. The future of the Gaelic League, at least as it had originally been envisaged, appeared in doubt.

Matters were only to get worse for Douglas Hyde. When the Abbey Theatre Company, under Augusta Gregory's leadership, was touring America in 1911, their performances of *Playboy of the Western World* by J. M. Synge caused riots at a number of theatres. Some members of audiences were affronted by the play's portrayal of Irish womanhood and Hyde was prevailed upon to soothe and appease the detractors. Inadvertently, in doing his best to help, Douglas let Lady Gregory down by what he said and displeased his good friend, John Quinn. His remarks struck the wrong chord and he soon realised that he had made the worst faux pas of his career. He felt he was losing his grip of the organisation and that his lifelong approach to the retention of speaking Irish was beginning to fall on deaf ears. Consequently he made up his mind to quit the Gaelic League, or at least its leadership, but he was encouraged to stay on, which he did reluctantly. He knew that forces within would be pushing him out as soon as possible. He wanted to resign gracefully rather than be ignominiously ejected from his position.

Before he eventually did go Douglas Hyde changed tack and began, in speeches throughout Ireland, to advocate independence by whatever means possible although he still said he preferred the constitutional approach. By mid 1914 the Home Rule Bill had been passed but had to be set in limbo on account of the outbreak of World War One which erupted on the world scene in August 1914. Douglas's hold on his League was further weakened when he attended the funeral at Glasnevin in August 1915 of the old Fenian, Jeremiah O'Donovan Rossa, whose body had been brought back from America. The spectacular events of that day were orchestrated by none other than Patrick Pearse, whose famous speech seemed to crystallise the minds of the huge crowds craning to hear what he had to say. Douglas Hyde, noting the fervour of the speech by Pearse, then made up his mind once and for all. At the Ard Fheis of the Gaelic League shortly after Rossa's funeral, he resigned as president. His resignation was accepted with much regret but he felt he had made the right decision. At age 55 he felt a great burden had been lifted from his worthy shoulders.

The Easter Rising

Douglas, his wife and daughters were at home at Earlsfort Place when the Rising broke out on Monday 24 April 1916. Along with Nuala and Una, he cycled around the city seeing and hearing some of the gunfire and early explosions. He assisted a friend of the family, Nellie O'Brien, by bringing her to their home owing to the danger she was experiencing at her own house which was close to the action. During the week he also had a gun and gun case confiscated by two policemen and two soldiers who did not issue a receipt. Knowing some of the senior personnel at Dublin Castle he set off in his Ford car and, having explained the matter to a sympathetic ear, he had his weapon returned to him. In retrospect Douglas had acted in a somewhat cavalier manner during what was a most dangerous situation in Dublin at that time.

When the rebels had surrendered and the leaders, including Patrick Pearse of course, been court martialled, Douglas's impression of the Rising was overall a positive one.

Post revolution and the Irish Free State

Back at Ratra Douglas and Lucy suffered the most terrible sadness when their elder daughter, Nuala, then aged 22, contracted TB and died on 30 September 1916. They were devastated and were further cruelly tried when Una, then 20, fell ill late in 1918 with scarlet fever and was hospitalised. They feared that she, too, had TB and were relieved at the diagnosis of scarlet fever. Una survived much to the relief and joy of her parents. It had been a frightful couple of years for the Hydes.

1921 was a most significant year for Ireland. The country had been partitioned and the Anglo-Irish talks, led by Arthur Griffith and Michael Collins, had led to a Treaty with Great Britain. Douglas agreed that the plenipotentiaries had done their best for to conclude a deal which, whilst not securing everything they had wanted, still gave the Free State a chance to move forward. The thought of reversion to a bloody war filled Douglas with fear and trembling. The Treaty was worth supporting.

When the Free State senate was formed, including as it did such luminaries as Willie Yeats, Douglas was most disappointed that he had not been chosen as a member. Many of his friends, led by Augusta Gregory, showed their disdain and continued to press for Douglas's appointment. He was finally co-opted in February 1925 to fill a vacancy but failed to retain his seat in the election of September 1925. Clearly Douglas Hyde was not the popular man he once was.

He now returned to his first love and that was teaching at the university. He revelled in the cut and thrust of the classroom and felt relieved that, finally, he had no more heavy responsibilities to bear. He was greatly respected by his students who affectionately nicknamed him 'Dougie'. He remained on the staff until his retirement in 1932. During these years he was elected to the Royal Irish Academy in 1929 and finally became president of the 'Hist' at Trinity in 1931.

Both Douglas and Lucy returned to Ratra after his retirement from the university. He loved being back amidst the countryside he had known all his early life and to be out shooting and fishing. Lucy never could bring herself to liking the home that her husband so enjoyed. They no longer made visits to Coole Park as Lady Gregory had died in May 1932. There were, however, plenty of visits from Una and her husband, James Sealy, and their children. Tranquil years seemed to lie ahead. But this proved not to be the case for yet another door opened for Douglas, by now well into his seventies.

Douglas Hyde – President of Ireland

By the end of 1937 Ireland had a new constitution and a President was an essential post to be filled. After many months of rumour and speculation Eamon de Valera's personal choice of Dr Douglas Hyde to fill the position of Ireland's first President was agreed unanimously. He was humbled at being asked to fulfil the role but gladly accepted. Before he ever took his place at Aras an Uachtarain (the former Viceroy's mansion in Phoenix Park) a number of important staff appointments had to be made. Michael MacDunphy was selected as secretary and his two ADCs were Basil Peterson and Eamon de Buitlear. The first arrangement to be made was for the President's inauguration to take place in St Patrick's Cathedral on 25 June 1938. This was a most moving and dignified service but one which was only attended by non-catholics. This meant that only Basil Peterson and a handful of ministers and officials were permitted to attend. By an edict of the Roman Catholic church, catholics were not permitted to enter the Anglican cathedral in those days before ecumenism had taken hold. Following the act of worship in St Patrick's, everyone made their way to St Patrick's Hall in Dublin Castle for the official swearing-in ceremony. This was again a stately and impressive ceremony, much of it conducted in Irish, with Douglas's daughter, Una, acting as the President's escort. Lucy Hyde never stayed at 'the Park', nor was she able, through ill health, to attend the various ceremonies that day. Then there was a short gathering at the castle with many representatives and dignitaries from different countries, although without any British official. Finally a splendid state dinner was held at the presidential mansion with all kinds of ambassadors, men and women from industry and the Papal Nuncio.

Life was exceedingly busy for the President whose enthusiasm for the job knew no bounds. He enjoyed meeting people or just repairing to the garden to talk to some of the staff there. He spent a great deal of time preparing speeches, something which rankled with MacDunphy who was a most punctilious man and who liked to write the President's speeches for him. Needless to say Douglas's informality made life awkward for his officials but they learned to live with their master's foibles. Annette, Douglas's sister, became his hostess, a responsibility she relished. Both of them loved talking to their visitors and making them feel at home.

Back in Ratra Lucy's health was clearly deteriorating and Douglas was not able to go to see her very often owing to his duties. There were faithful men and women at Ratra to care for Lucy so she was well attended in that regard. Lucy became very ill just before Christmas 1938 and, immediately after making his first Christmas address to the people, Douglas hurried off to Frenchpark. There Lucy, his partner of 45 years, died on New Year's Eve 1938. She was buried in the little churchyard at Portahard alongside her daughter, Nuala, and other members of Douglas's family. In the following spring the President, in the company of de Buitlear, spent time at Ratra where Douglas was still able to indulge in his favourite sport of shooting and fishing. Over this period Douglas got to know de Buitlear well and grew to greatly like him. The feeling was mutual.

When World War Two broke out in September 1939, Douglas was in full agreement with de Valera and his decision to remain neutral during the conflict. He continued to undertake many presidential duties until he suffered a stroke in April 1940, aged 80. His right side was affected but not his speech so, apart from being in a wheelchair, he still could vigorously pursue his tasks. His enthusiasm never waned and he simply came to terms with not being able to use his legs. He participated in countless events which required his presidential presence including one which particularly pleased him. This was the 50th anniversary, in 1943, of the founding of the Gaelic League. This proved to be a nostalgic evening meeting many of his former colleagues some of whom had not seen him for years.

In 1945, as the war was coming to a conclusion, Douglas's seven year spell as President came to an end. He was asked to remain for a second term as permitted by the constitution, but, being already 85, he declined the offer. He made his preparations to leave 'the Park' including the distribution of gifts to all his staff. The country reciprocated by allowing him to live in a smaller building in Phoenix Park which was renamed 'Little Ratra' in his honour. In 1947 he presented Ratra house itself to the Gaelic League but nothing ever came of this and the house, having fallen into disrepair, had its roof removed shortly afterwards. It was a sad end to such an iconic and much loved home of Douglas Hyde.

Dr Douglas Hyde, first President of Ireland, lover of the Irish language, poet and playwright, died peacefully on 12 July 1949, just six months short of his 90th birthday. On 14 July his cortege made its way back to St Patrick's Cathedral for the funeral service according to the Church of Ireland prayer book and, once again, sitting huddled in their cars during the service, sat Eamon de Valera and his ministers, still not allowed to participate in the obsequies for their beloved country's first President. At the conclusion of the service, the funeral cars made their way through the centre of Ireland to that little Portahard churchyard where he was laid to rest alongside his wife and his family. Douglas Hyde's earthly journey was over.

This gentle giant of a man who had inspired so many of his countrymen and women throughout his long life is remembered today in that little church in the Roscommon countryside now turned into a Douglas Hyde museum. A statue of the great man overlooks the graveyard where countless people visit his plot each year. Ireland would do well to remember the legacy of such a towering scion of Irish history.

Suggested reading

1. Daly, Dominic, *The Young Douglas Hyde*, Dublin, 1974.
2. Dunleavy, Janet & Gareth, *Douglas Hyde – a Maker of Modern Ireland*, California and Oxford, 1991.

Erskine Childers

Enigmatic and conscientious – a zealous convert

His early life

There can scarcely be anyone, even today in the early 21st century, who has not heard of the novel *The Riddle of the Sands*. The novel, written in 1903, has sold countless millions of copies and has been reprinted dozens of times. It has also been made into a film, most recently in 1984 starring Michael York, Simon McCorkindale and Jenny Agutter. It is a story of espionage and intrigue, of courage and derring-do. The author was Robert Erskine Childers, always known as Erskine, and he was born on 25 June 1870 in London, the second of five children of Robert and Anna Childers. His mother was a Barton of Annamoe in county Wicklow, thus making young Erskine half Irish, a fact which was to play a crucial role throughout his life.

Erskine had an older brother, Henry, and three younger sisters, Constance, Dulcibella and Sybil. Their father, Robert, was a learned man and an oriental scholar. The family boasted a number of influential ancestors some of whom took Holy Orders, including his grandfather, Charles Childers. Robert was a most active man but sadly, at the early age of 38, he contracted tuberculosis and died. Erskine was just six years old and his sisters even younger. Anna their mother, struggled to keep the family together. Although she seemed healthy enough, she was sent to an isolation hospital for fear of having TB herself and died in 1883 when Erskine was only 13 years old. Not only was she cruelly confined to a hospital ward but she was also denied the right to see her own children. The children had been cared for by family and servants in England during their mother's hospitalisation. When she died yet another crisis of weighty proportions hung like a sword of Damocles over the now orphaned youngsters and that was what was to become of them.

A ready and most suitable solution, however, was quickly found. Their relatives, Robert and Agnes Barton, from county Wicklow came to the rescue. They invited the Childers children to come and live with them in their lovely ascendancy house, which was called 'Glendalough House' but known to the family simply and affectionately as 'Glan'. Although this was a typically extensive gentry house, an extension had to be built to accommodate the five new arrivals. The Bartons, who had five children of their own, proved wonderful and endearing foster parents to the Childers brood and seemed to think nothing of an overnight increase in their family of 100%. There were, of course, many nannies and staff to help look after them all, but it was surely a selfless undertaking. Never would any of the Childers youngsters forget the immense sacrifice made by their aunt and uncle. Erskine would remain close to his aunt Agnes throughout his life.

The children knew 'Glan' very well, having spent summer holidays there and they enjoyed the pursuits of the ascendancy classes like horse riding, shooting and hunting. Erskine, though ten years older than his cousin, Robert Barton, became very close to him and they remained like brothers throughout their lives. The village of Annamoe, in that beautiful part of county Wicklow near the Vale of Avoca and the Meeting of the Waters, is situated close to the neighbouring village of Rathdrum, where the famous Parnell family lived in their Avondale home. The families of course were well acquainted with one another and there were regular comings and goings between them.

School and university and life back in England
On the recommendation of his grandfather, Canon Charles Childers, Erskine was soon packed off to public school in England. Haileybury, in Hertfordshire in England, was the choice and Erskine was enrolled in 1883 at the age of 13. There he remained, making steady progress and making friends, for almost seven years until he won a scholarship to Trinity College, Cambridge. He was greatly involved in college activities including their debating society, the 'Magpie and Stump', and the prestigious college newspaper, *Cambridge Review* of which he became editor. Erskine was never a great debater, hindered by his hoity-toity accent and his poor oratory. Having read law he graduated with First Class Honours. His university days had been well spent.

However, rather than pursuing a career as a lawyer, Erskine decided on the civil service and consequently sat the civil service entrance examination. Out of hundreds of candidates he came third and applied for, and was successful in landing, an important job as a committee clerk in the House of Commons. His task for the next eleven years was to draft acts of parliament. In this position Erskine Childers was well thought of and respected. The tight discipline of his job was to stand him in good stead for the rest of his life. And the post had its distinct advantages. Depending on the length of the parliamentary sittings his time off on holiday could be very generous. He worked hard when the Commons was in session, but he was to play hard when he had time off to pursue his own special interest.

His passion for sailing

Erskine Childers may have been serious and bookish in his job in the Commons, but when he took to his hobby, his personality completely changed. He loved sailing from his youngest days around the shores of England and Ireland and over the years owned a number of small sailing craft. He had learnt to master the waves as a young man around the shores of the Solent and the relatively quiet waters off the English coast. He often sailed alone but would also have had, as companion on board ship, his brother, Henry, or one of his small circle of friends. His favourite destination was the Friesian islands off the coast of Germany. Navigating his shallow draft boats in these mysterious waters around the islands of Norderney, Juist and Borkum was his chief delight. He loved plying in and out of the little islands and their harbours. The mists, which constantly hung over their sandy beaches, only added to the secrecy of what he might discover as he investigated these shores. The islands were soon to provide the genus of the book he would write and which would become, not only a best seller amongst a public eager and willing to read his story of intrigue, but also a 'must read' novel for leaders of the nations on either side of the North Sea determined upon springing nasty surprises on one another. Whilst captain of his little vessel, Erskine Childers became the veritable despot, or at least so said his friends who became not simply deckhands but effectively galley slaves. He was as a man possessed on board his ship and would brook no slacking from his crew. But, it should also be said, he never had any difficulty in persuading his friends to join him, tyrant or no tyrant.

For Queen and country

In the last days of Queen Victoria's reign, the Boer War broke out between the mighty British Empire and the little South African republics. The Empire may have eventually won, but it certainly received a very bloody nose. Into this conflict, in 1899, Erskine Childers readily joined. He had no hesitation in signing up into the Honourable Artillery Company to be attached to the C.I.V., the City Imperial Volunteers. Despite his poor eyesight, necessitating his wearing glasses, and a sciatic leg, Childers, and his best friend, Basil Williams, set off by ship for Cape Town. His initial job on board was to take care of the horses, a not inconsiderable task on such a lengthy sea voyage. On arrival Childers soon saw action and was close to some of the bitterest fighting between the skilful Boer guerrilla fighters and the swathes of British soldiers replete in their colourful, but all too conspicuous, uniforms. By sheer force of numbers, and regardless of the thousands of soldiers killed and injured, the British eventually won through. It had probably been the first occasion when the mighty men in red were almost defeated by a band of crafty fighters hiding in the hills and constantly surprising their enemy.

Erskine Childers may have been a proud British soldier, and he was decorated for his part in the battles, but he secretly admired the tactics of the Boers and their worthy leaders like Botha, de Wet and Kruger. He would go on later in his life to participate in such a guerrilla campaign in Ireland. And he also saw the useful part played by the Irish Brigade led by Major John MacBride on behalf of the Boer republics. MacBride was also to have a most colourful life having firstly married Maud Gonne in 1904 and then being executed after the 1916 Easter Rising in Dublin. Childers, as ever, took note.

Upon his return from an exhausting war, Childers took to writing. In 1901, he wrote his first book *In the Ranks of the C.I.V.*. This was basically a book for army consumption in which he suggested a radical change in the tactics of HM forces and even inferred criticism of the method of fighting campaigns such as the one recently contested in South Africa. It was time, high time, to reconsider the entire strategy of facing enemies in the future. Lines of red-coated soldiers taking to the field to fight an enemy could no longer be the sensible tactic by which to overwhelm the opposition. Despite his criticisms, Childers was commended for his book, even by some senior Army grandees.

Within a year or so came his most popular novel *The Riddle of the Sands*. It was an instant success being sought after by people from every part of the globe. Interestingly, politicians and senior army personnel not only in Britain, but also by commanders throughout an increasingly jittery Europe were reading it. The theme of the novel was one of espionage and intrigue with the very real possibility of any country using the misty low-lying Friesian islands to prepare an all out attack on either side of the North Sea. By dint of using shallow-hulled boats any possible aggressor could secretly prepare for an invasion leaving its enemy completely in ignorance. More and more were the national leaders convinced by the plan drawn up by this intriguer-in-chief, Erskine Childers.

Marriage and beyond

Not long after returning from South Africa and the conflict there the Honourable Artillery Company was invited to visit Boston. There were contrary opinions as to the efficacy of such a trip owing to many American voices which still saw the British Empire in general, and Britain in particular, as being the enemy. However the majority of citizens in that city were delighted at the prospect of such a prestigious regiment visiting. It would be an opportunity for the Americans to put on a show and for the soldiers to excel. And so it proved. Childers had been specifically earmarked by the top brass in the regiment to be an integral part of the company. *The Riddle of the Sands* had been a popular read amongst the army and he accepted the invitation with alacrity.

In Boston there were all sorts of dinners and engagements for the visitors to accept and, at one of these evenings, Childers happened to sit down beside Molly Osgood whose father was an influential Bostonian. It was love at first sight. Childers was, by now, 33 years old and he freely admitted that meeting the beautiful Molly had swept him off his feet. The Osgoods were keen on Ireland and had definite views rather more on the nationalist side than on that of the Crown. This did not faze Erskine who very soon after meeting Molly, proposed to her and they were married in January 1904.

Molly Osgood had a very complicated life story. She had been injured whilst skating as a young child of three and had been virtually confined to a wheelchair. It looked as if she would never walk again but, through guts and determination, and of course by dint of the surgeon's skill, an operation when she was in her teenage years restored her mobility. Later still further surgery enabled her to bear children. And then, in her mid twenties, she met Erskine Childers, married him and was his boon companion for the rest of his life. As a belated wedding present, the Osgood parents presented the young couple with a sailing boat, the *Asgard*, which was to play a vital part in the life of Erskine Childers.

Here then was Erskine Childers returning to London with a wife after a relatively brief stay in the eastern United States. Molly and he took up residence in a flat in London and Erskine went back to his job at Westminster. For the next number of months he introduced his new wife to his friends and family and everyone found Molly adorable and friendly. However she herself found the transition from affluent Boston to rich and comfortable London society somewhat difficult to handle. In due course however, she overcame her worries and settled in.

Molly and Erskine were soon sailing their new boat in the seas, so well known to Erskine, around the English coast and, of course, through those mysterious Dutch and German Friesian islands across the North Sea. Despite her not yet complete mobility, Molly was to grow into a most accomplished sailor and, like all his crews before him, happily bent to her husband's punishing schedule as a ship's captain.

In December 1905 their son, Erskine Hamilton Childers, was born and he brought great joy to both his parents. A couple of years later they lost another son but, in 1910, their younger son, Robert Alden, was born. Their family was complete and a great bond was established between parents and sons over the succeeding years.

By the year of his second son's birth, 1910, Erskine Childers had decided to resign as a committee clerk to concentrate on his writing. His books and his regular pamphlets had been popular and he was in great demand. He wrote a number of documents for the army and was commended for them. He continued to be critical of British tactics following his experiences in South Africa. Rather than putting the army chiefs off by his comments and suggestions Childers continued to attract work. He had obviously made the right move.

His conversion to the Irish cause

It should never be forgotten that Erskine Childers was half Irish. Ireland, and his loving relatives in county Wicklow, had always played an important role in his life. After all the Bartons had rescued the Childers children from the possibility of having their family broken up after the death, in such sad circumstances, of their mother. Erskine had formed a strong bond with his aunt at 'Glan' and particularly with Robert, his younger cousin. Ireland, by the end of the first decade of the twentieth century, had once more found itself in the melting pot. Separation from the British, by fair means or foul, was on the cards. The Bartons, regardless of their Anglo-Irish ascendancy background, were firmly on the side of those who wanted to force the British out of Ireland by non-constitutional methods. Robert was a convert to Home Rule and joined those demanding a British withdrawal. And Erskine Childers was beginning to form the same impression. He had seen the way that the British had treated the Boers and, although he had freely fought for Queen and country in that debacle in southern Africa, he too saw that the time had come for a radical change. And he was now determined to join in the campaign.

In 1910, a very busy year for him, Childers had written his first non-fiction book, the hard-hitting *The Framework of Home Rule*. He vehemently made the case for Ireland to be free from Britain and for it no longer to be treated simply as an appendage. The book proved the case for an Ireland separate from Britain and it brought a great many plaudits from all over the British Isles and beyond.

When the Ulster Volunteers ran illegal weapons into the north in 1914, many in the south demanded action too. Thus were formed the Irish Volunteers under the leadership of the scholarly Eoin MacNeill. The truth is that many southerners admired the action of Carson and his men who had no love for Home Rule and opposed any separation from Great Britain. Many said it was a strange way to pursue their aims by threatening to fight against the very government from which they never wanted to be separated.

If the Ulstermen had guns, then the Irish Volunteers needed them too. They wanted money to purchase the weapons and they required transport to bring their illegal cargo into Ireland. And so Erskine Childers entered the frame. The well-known Darrell Figgis approached Childers knowing that he was sympathetic to the cause and what was more, he owned a boat which could be used to bring the arms into Ireland. Without a moment's hesitation, he agreed to offer the *Asgard* for the mission. He accompanied Figgis to Germany where the deal was done and around 1500 guns and ammunition were purchased. Much has been said about the quality (not to mention the quantity) of the weapons bought but, although they were pretty ancient, they at least worked and, above all, the Irish could be assured of being at least partly prepared for whatever outcome would emerge.

Arrangements were made for the boat to be manned and the crew included Molly Childers and Mary Spring Rice, a member of the old Anglo-Irish ascendancy herself. After a tricky expedition, more than half of the guns were brought into Howth, north of Dublin, on 26 July 1914. The remaining weapons were brought into Kilcoole in county Wicklow the next week on the yacht *Kelpie* which was owned and skippered by Conor O'Brien. Although the Howth gun running passed almost without incident, there was a sting in the tail when three civilians were killed and many injured by British soldiers trying to disrupt those bringing the guns into Dublin. This became known locally as the 'Bachelor's Walk massacre'.

Childers, not yet so well known in and around Dublin at the time, soon became quite a celebrity amongst those who had joined the cause. But then the world found itself at war. The Irish question was quickly relegated into the background. Many thousands of young Irishmen, from the north and from the south, enlisted to fight on the side of the Crown. Independence and guns and disruption gave way to service in the army or the navy. And another who had been totally immersed in the recent shadowy activities soon did the same. Erskine Childers left Dublin and enlisted in His Majesty's forces as a lieutenant in the Naval Air Arm at Felixstowe. The cause of Ireland now took a back seat. The cause of Britain and its allies took immediate precedence. There was never any question of wondering whether or not to join up. Erskine Childers knew where he was needed and that was on the King's side.

Service in World War One

Having expended so much of his energy on the nationalist cause in recent times, Childers now engaged in frenetic activity during the years of the First World War, 1914-1918. Becoming a volunteer in the embryonic air force meant difficult and incredibly dangerous times for Childers. He became an observer on a seaplane which patrolled the seas off the south east coast of England. However it should be remembered that a seaplane in 1914 was something very different from the sophisticated aircraft of today. The sorties carried out by the brave crews were of extreme importance to the way the war was being prosecuted. Childers and his fellow enlisted men and officers took part in a most critical raid over the town of Cuxhaven in the early months of the conflict. A great deal of vital information was elicited from this courageous flight and, for his part in it, Erskine Childers was mentioned in dispatches.

Hardly had he got used to the vagaries of flying in aircraft than Childers was transferred to *HMS Ben My Chree* and sent to the Dardanelles in the eastern Mediterranean. This was a contrast of some proportion and so he had to adjust to becoming a navy man as opposed to an air force one. In this humbling and deadly field of operation Childers played his part and was indeed fortunate to come out of it alive considering the thousands of British who were slaughtered on those forbidding rocks on the Black Sea. By 1917 he had returned to England to find himself the proud recipient of a DSO (the Distinguished Service Order).

After these three long and testing years in uniform, Childers found himself with a completely different kind of occupation from the summer of 1917. But before taking up this next posting, he, like the rest of the country, had to try to come to terms with the aftermath of the 1916 Easter Rising in Dublin. In his schizophrenic state, Childers found himself in a dilemma. He was fighting on the side of King and country, and most bravely too, yet he had already been smitten by the nationalist bug. His cousin, Robert Barton, had also, although like Erskine in British uniform, become an out and out republican. Dilemmas are there to be solved, so thought Childers, but still he had work to do before the war would eventually end in 1918. And this was work for that part of him which continued to be a loyal subject of Britain.

In the months following the Easter Rising when the leaders of that insurrection, Patrick Pearse et al, had acted so decisively in an Irish opportunity during an English difficulty, the British Prime Minister, David Lloyd George, moved to resolve the Irish problem once and for all. He set up a convention in Dublin to which he invited the various protagonists to sit down with each other to sort out the future of Ireland. It was a tall order after 700 years of British rule yet it seemed to Lloyd George that Irishmen talking would be an infinitely better idea than them continuing to fight. However there were immediate obstacles. The newly resurgent 'Sinn Feiners' refused to join and the unionists from the north only participated reluctantly. And, of course, not one single woman was invited to be one of the 100 delegates.

In the preparations for the administration of the convention, an order was sent to Erskine Childers to act as one of the secretaries. His reputation as a writer and editor had gone before him and he seemed an ideal choice for the role. And so he took up residence in Dublin only seeing his wife and family whenever he had an opportunity. His family life had, of course, been severely disrupted by his war service and he had missed many of the early stages in his sons' lives. From the late summer of 1917 until the spring of 1918, he remained with the squabbling delegates to the convention and undertook his responsibilities in his usual punctilious manner. But he was glad to be finished and even looked for a chance to get back to war service. The war to end all wars continued to lumber onwards until the armistice was eventually signed in November. But before it was all over Erskine Childers had yet another part to play in the last months of the war. He joined coastal intelligence and, during this time, he suffered the loss of one of his greatest friends, Gordon Shephard, who had been often aboard Childers' various sailing vessels on their journeys to the Friesian islands. It was a devastating blow not only for Childers but also for Molly who had been very close to Shephard herself.

And so the war ended. Childers had fought bravely; he had been decorated for his part in the conflict; he had fought fearlessly for King and country. He was now 48 years old and his health was deteriorating. His sciatic leg was giving him trouble and his bodily frame was broken. He looked more like 78 than 48. By the time he was at last mustered out of HM forces it was March 1919. He had done his duty, and in a remarkably brave manner, but his mindset had changed. He now clearly saw Ireland as his life's work. He now had to convince Molly to pursue the same goals and move to live in, and work for, Ireland.

The die is cast

Childers was now determined to move to Dublin and pursue the Irish cause. There were, however, a number of obstacles to overcome. This archetypal Englishman, with his supercilious manner and upper class accent, was going to have problems convincing the Irish rank and file that he was on their side. The Irish had, clearly enough, seen his convictions in practice when he ran the guns into Howth just as war was breaking out. Yet they also saw that he had readily joined up and fought for Britain during the war and wondered what side he really would support.

Childers arrived in Dublin as soon as he had been demobbed. He arrived with a purpose. He went straight to the door of Arthur Griffith and Sinn Fein and offered his services. In many ways they could hardly refuse after all the work and energy he had put into the gun running; they could hardly deny that Childers exhibited glowing credentials; they could hardly afford to turn away such an enthusiastic supporter. But they had their misgivings, especially Griffith. So he gave Childers a testing job to do. Perhaps it was his way of convincing himself that this exuberant Englishman did have a part to play in the new Ireland. The task set for Childers suited him down to the ground. He was asked to publish a paper called *The Irish Bulletin*. Under trying circumstances Childers successfully published this newssheet five days a week for almost two years.

He had not only to raise the articles for the editions but had also to arrange for its regular publication often in very difficult conditions. But Griffith and his diffident and suspicious colleagues quickly came to appreciate that Erskine Childers was a man of his word and also possibly the hardest working man they had yet come across.

Molly Childers took some persuading to make the permanent move to Dublin from London, which she had come to like since her arrival from the United States in 1904. She felt that Erskine's ascendancy background and pompous accent would go against him although she had to admit that her husband seemed to have overcome these problems with the work he had already been doing. She soon agreed, therefore, to take this momentous decision and arrived in Dublin by the autumn of 1919. From then on she was entirely behind what Erskine was doing and it was not long until she herself was just as enthusiastic and involved as her husband was. Molly and Erskine, man and wife, became veritable powerhouses for the Irish cause. They were never to turn back or have any doubts. They had made their beds and they would lie in them.

By 1919, not long after the 'Khaki' election of December 1918, the Irish members elected had decided not to take their seats at Westminster so they set up their own Dail, their own government. Illegal as of course it was it met regularly with as many of its members as were still at liberty. Many others were in prison following the arrests which were becoming commonplace in Ireland at the time. Desmond Fitzgerald (the father of Garret) had been appointed Director of Communications in the Dail. But he was arrested and into his place was slotted none other than Erskine Childers. He seemed an obvious choice but more and more the likes of Arthur Griffith grew to dislike him because of his meticulous habits. On the other hand Eamon de Valera and Childers got on well, at least when de Valera was around in Dublin and not either in jail or in America.

Another friend Molly and Erskine made was Michael Collins. This young dynamo was just the sort of man who excited them and Molly involved herself in helping Collins with the collection of money for the National Loan. This money was distributed to those whose lives had been disrupted by what they saw as the British menace and their bullyboy tactics of destroying the homes and farms of the Irish.

Almost by way of proving himself to the doubting republicans, Childers himself was arrested at the time of the truce in June 1921, but he was quickly released. At this juncture the dreaded Anglo-Irish War or the War of Independence ended leaving further room for yet another chance to get the British and the Irish to talk over the table. Erskine Childers would now get an opportunity to participate in these negotiations, but not exactly in the way he himself would have wanted.

Treaty negotiations

By now Childers was totally immersed in Irish life and there could be no turning back. Despite his rather haughty English persona, he had been of great and true worth to de Valera and even to Griffith who continued to be more than suspicious of him. After the truce had been agreed the first thing that de Valera did was to accept an invitation from London to attend upon David Lloyd George there to enter into discussions about the future of Ireland. This call to Downing Street was significant for never before had a British Prime Minister taken time to talk seriously to the Irish. So de Valera travelled to London and in his party was Erskine Childers. He had been taken as a secretary mainly at de Valera's insistence. He accepted that the person who could help him most on constitutional matters was Childers. De Valera had come to rely on Childers' judgement on such matters. The talks themselves, however, proved inconclusive and, if the truth were told, they became simply a talking shop between de Valera and Lloyd George with the remainder of the negotiating team basically shut out from all discussions.

When de Valera returned to Dublin he had little to show for his time spent with the British Prime Minister. Childers was, of course, disappointed that nothing had been promised and nothing decided that would further the case for Irish independence. And his skills, therefore, had not been put to the test.

There was, however, a continuing swell of optimism that some kind of deal could be done with the British. They were still struggling in their own back yard to improve the lot of the British people after the disastrous world war and so it seemed reasonable to think that if they could make peace with the Irish then at least one of their headaches would have been settled. In October a team of Irish negotiators assembled to return to London to continue the talks started by de Valera in the summer. De Valera chose not to lead the party himself and so it was led by Griffith and Collins. In this team of five was included Childers' cousin, Robert Barton. And, as chief secretary, Erskine Childers was chosen. Deep down he considered that he himself should have been part of the negotiating team but this was hardly likely to have happened. However he was there and he hoped to be able to influence the thinking of the Irish delegates.

As the talks progressed Griffith's attitude to Childers did not change. He had not wanted him to be there even in the role as chief secretary. As the weeks went by Childers became almost ostracised and Griffith even considered that Childers was a spy for de Valera. He certainly was not but his views and thoughts certainly reciprocated those of the leader back in Dublin. Childers did not cover himself in glory at the talks. He was too self-opinionated which led to the talks breaking into a series of sub conferences which kept out secretarial staff, including, of course, Childers himself. The talks, after much debate and pressure from the British side, proved to be fairly successful and the plenipotentiaries (as they had been appointed) were ready to come back to Dublin with, if not everything that they wanted, at least enough to move matters forward. There had been acrimonious discussions amongst the team members and with Childers, their chief secretary, who was at total odds with the agreement. The leadership shown by Griffith and Collins was decisive and they were able to bring the doubters, mainly Barton, to the agreement.

When they returned to Dublin it was a different matter with de Valera and his cronies, Stack and Brugha, totally up in arms against the treaty signed in London. The Dail strenuously debated the issues before and after Christmas and, in the end, those who supported the treaty won out by 64 votes to 57. De Valera immediately resigned and he remained in the political wilderness for some years to come. Childers, himself a TD (MP), voted against the treaty too and soon afterwards Robert Barton was to repudiate the agreement as well.

These demanding days, weeks and months continued to take their toll on Erskine Childers' health. He had aged dramatically and he looked a wreck. Needless to say he continued to push himself too hard which only made matters worse. Any pleas from Molly for him to relax and rest for even a short period fell on deaf ears. He was like a man possessed. As it soon proved he had not much longer to live.

The civil war and its tragic aftermath

Although the Irish people eventually got the chance to vote three to one in favour of the treaty (in effect in favour of peace principally), the worst possible outcome for Ireland was presaged. A tragic civil war broke out in the summer of 1922 inevitably setting brother against brother and father against son. Childers immediately left Dublin to join the IRA and was appointed a staff captain. He kept closely aligned with Eamon de Valera and was given yet another challenging task. This time he was expected to publish a weekly edition of *An Phoblacht* which was the war news for the Republican forces. During this odious internecine struggle he had to find copy, to publish and to distribute this newssheet which became incredibly difficult especially when Childers found himself having to lead a donkey and cart loaded with his printing paraphernalia through the mountains of county Cork. It was a thankless undertaking.

All the while the Free State government, now led by W. T. Cosgrave and Kevin O'Higgins following the deaths of Griffith and Collins in August 1922, was pursuing, with vigour and determination, those who opposed them. They introduced punitive legislation which included the certainty of a death sentence for anyone found carrying arms and ammunition. They stuck to their guns in an effort to keep the new state on the rails. This law was now to work against Erskine Childers.

By now Childers, on the run for some months, was a marked man. O'Higgins, as minister of Home Affairs, was determined to make an example of him. Childers knew this; Molly knew it too. She pleaded with her husband to flee the country while he still had the chance. Childers resolutely refused to leave. It seemed that he realised that, with a price on his head, the sands of time were running out. As he struggled through the hills in all kinds of weather and to continue to produce his paper, though with increasing difficulty, the Free State forces were closing in. De Valera, having managed to reach Dublin, now summoned Childers to the capital to take over as Secretary of State in the Dail administration. Childers, weaker and more disabled than ever, saw this posting as a poisoned chalice but he had little choice. He and de Valera had remained close even in the shocking conditions of mountain survival and he resolved to accept the job.

With great difficulty he escaped the rigours of the Cork mountains and made his way towards Dublin. And then he made a crucial mistake if, in fact, it was a blunder at all. He arrived at 'Glan' at Annamoe. He felt safe there yet he must have realised the danger he was in. He had deliberately not gone to his appointed safe house. 'Glan' was bound to have been under close surveillance and, as it happened, it surely was. He had only been at his childhood home for a day or two when the inevitable knock came on the door late one night. The callers forced an entry and demanded to see Childers. It must have been a tip off. Erskine Childers had been betrayed. As he was searched, the little pearl-handled gun which Michael Collins had given him, was discovered in his pocket. The Free State forces now knew their chance had come and Childers was arrested and brought to Dublin, after spending a night in nearby Wicklow jail.

O'Higgins had, of course, been informed of Childers' capture. He was cock-a-hoop yet he knew the delicate position he was in. The law on possessing weapons had been enacted but no one had yet been charged and, what is imperative, no one had as yet been sentenced to death. What was he to do? He consulted Cosgrave and his cabinet colleagues and listened to the arguments for and against making Childers the scapegoat. As there were men already charged with similar offences, O'Higgins made a fateful decision. He brought four young men from their prison cells and had them executed at Kilmainham jail, as he said, ' pour encourager les autres'. They were put to death on 17 November 1922.

The stage was set for the court martial of Erskine Childers, the number one thorn in the flesh for the Free State government. Although there was a lengthy hearing before the appointed judges, Childers was sentenced to death for the possession of a weapon contrary to the law recently passed and enacted. He was put to death by firing squad on 24 November at Beggar's Bush Barracks, just a week after those first four executions. As he stood awaiting death, typically he refused a blindfold and even encouraged his executioners to stand a little nearer to him to make their job easier. And, true to the form of this enigmatic Englishman and Irish Republican zealot, he came forward and shook hands with all the men who, moments later, fired the shots that sent him to eternity. He had written to his wife reaffirming his deep love for her and his sons, then just 17 and 12 years old respectively, and seeking their forgiveness. She surely forgave him and, for the rest of her life until her death in 1964, she stood by her husband's ideals and never wavered from the goals he had set for himself in his striving for an Ireland totally free from the British yoke. Why had he carried the gun? Perhaps it was his way of ensuring that he died the martyr's death in the way Irishmen had done for so long. Maybe he thought that his would be the last such death. Erskine Childers was an enigma, of that there is no doubt. He was intelligent and able. He had fought for King and country in two gruelling wars and had been decorated for his bravery. He was an author of note. But his greatest aspiration was his fanatical espousal, even if it did come in his later years, to the cause of Irish independence which led him to sacrifice his very life for the country he loved.

Suggested reading

1. Boyle, Andrew, *The Riddle of Erskine Childers*, London, 1977.
2. Childers, Erskine, *The Riddle of the Sands*, London, from 1903.
3. Ring, Jim, *Erskine Childers, Author of the Riddle of the Sands*, London, 1996.
4. Wilkinson, Burke, *The Zeal of the Convert – the Life of Erskine Childers*, Washington, 1976.

The O'Rahilly

Assiduous and able – the brains behind the Easter Rising

To those who know the story of the 1916 Easter Rising, the names of Patrick Pearse, Tom Clarke and James Connolly immediately spring to mind. Yet the contribution of one remarkable man, who to this day remains rather in the shadows, ought never to be forgotten. Michael Joseph Rahilly was significantly involved in the planning and preparation for this seminal event in Ireland's long and turbulent history – this rebellion which lasted barely six days and yet which led to independence for the majority of the counties in Ireland in 1921.

A birth in county Kerry

Michael Rahilly was born on 21 April 1875 in the little north Kerry town of Ballylongford situated close to the southern banks of the river Shannon. It never ranked as a very important town in that county although it was near the county town, Listowel, just nine miles distant. The boy was the third and last child, and only son, of Richard and Ellen (nee Mangan). His older sisters were Nell and Anna.

The Rahillys were a prosperous family in that part of county Kerry and Richard, Michael's father, was a man of note in the town. He owned and ran an extensive hardware business which he had inherited from his own father. The shop was a focal point in Ballylongford and was the sort of establishment which was able to provide many essential and useful items for the citizens of the town and surrounding countryside. There were other wealthy aunts and uncles of the Rahilly family in the town who had also done well in life. Richard, apart from his business acumen, dealt in stocks and shares and was an inventor to boot. He invented a cash register and was unfortunate not to have achieved the patent for the machine. He was interested in making artificial ice and nearly owned a factory which would have made it. He was a man of extraordinary talent and this flare he passed on to his son.

The Rahillys were also a respectable family who took their public responsibilities very seriously. They were an ardent and bourgeois Roman Catholic family who fitted in with the establishment in their area. Richard Rahilly was a Justice of the Peace and was one of the first catholics to have been so honoured. Dublin Castle had evidently considered the Rahillys to be both reputable and well thought of. In due course of time young Michael would also hold a similar position. They were never, at that stage at any rate, a political family and, although they were nationalists, they never raised any concern amongst the authorities.

In the history of the family over the years there appeared a number of significant gaps. Little is known of Ellen, Michael's mother, which seems strange considering the prominence of the family in north Kerry. In later years, however, Mrs Rahilly did make her mark in settling her only son's future.

Michael's early life and influences

Michael attended the local national school in Ballylongford. This was a deliberate policy of his parents to send their son to be educated amongst the local children. There was no wish to have him sent away at an early age or be educated at home by governesses. He was always grateful for the opportunity to savour teaching in his own town and he was able to have the chance to learn the Irish language which, whilst falling out of favour in many parts of Ireland, was still spoken in county Kerry. This interest and fascination for the language remained with him throughout his life. As a child he also was keen on playing the piano and his greatest hobby was making handcrafts. He enjoyed his early days at school. However in 1890 when he was 15 years old, he was sent off to the prestigious Jesuit boarding school, Clongowes, in county Kildare. He received a typical middle class catholic education amidst learned and intelligent teacher priests. He did well at Clongowes, winning many prizes and participating in the Irish sports played at the school. Above all he made many friends, some of whom would turn up in his later life as well. In 1893 he left Clongowes and headed for the Royal University in Dublin to study medicine.

In the same year Michael Rahilly met his future wife. He was just 18 years old and his newfound love barely into her teenage years. Nannie Brown was one of five sisters whose father had recently died. They came from Philadelphia and had come, shortly after Mr Brown's death, to spend a holiday in county Clare. Their mother had considered that it would be advantageous for her daughters to take time away from America where they could experience the peace and tranquillity of Ireland. They had an enjoyable time in the west of Ireland and it was during this time that a party had been arranged by their hosts and to this event an invitation had been sent to Michael. He immediately fell in love with Nannie although he must have realised that their chances of staying together were remote. But, as the saying goes, the course of true love never did run smooth. The Browns soon left Ireland to visit Paris and, by that time, Michael had only met Nannie once or twice. But he was a determined young man. He set off for Paris himself with a view to pursuing his romance with Nannie. It was a costly outing but he knew that he was doing the right thing. Nannie, who was studying in the French capital with her sisters, was surprised to see Michael although they had been corresponding. He returned home firmly resolved to marry Nannie Brown.

Michael resumed his medical studies in Dublin but, in 1894, he contracted tuberculosis, an all too common affliction at the end of the nineteenth century. He was sent home from Clongowes to recuperate and there his mother and sisters nursed him back to health. He had had a close call for he knew perfectly well that many people died from the disease. He then made another decision. He would not return to university and so gave up any hope of becoming a doctor. In truth he had never been very keen on the profession and realised he had not had a calling to practise medicine. He spent his time helping out his father in his business with a view to working out how he should proceed in life.

Great sadness was visited upon the Rahilly household on 24 March 1896. Richard Rahilly died of pneumonia that day leaving the future of the family business up in the air. His mother had been left Richard's entire estate and she became a reasonably wealthy woman. She decided to leave Ballylongford to take up residence in a former gentry house, Quinsborough, over the border in county Limerick. Michael was simply expected to run the business and get on with serving the community as his father and grandfather had done before him. This idea was not, however, to his liking. He did not consider himself a businessman. But he had a problem. If he gave up running the store, he would not have any income for he was financially dependent on his mother. If he was to get on in life and if he was to marry his Nannie, he needed a regular allowance.

It was not long, therefore, until he headed over to Quinsborough to face his mother with his dilemma. She had, of course, assumed that her son would have been happy to run the business and make money from it to keep himself solvent. When Michael sat down for his tête-à-tête with his mother he firmly explained to her that he did not want to continue running the store and that it would have to be sold. And what was more, he demanded a regular allowance from the proceeds of the sale. His mother understood his determination and agreed to put the business on the market. It sold without much bother and an arrangement was made between mother and son for a handsome payment to be made to him for the rest of his life. The amount was indeed very generous which meant that Michael Rahilly did not have to earn any money from then on. This meant that when he got involved in every kind of endeavour throughout the remainder of his life, he had time to concentrate on the matter in hand. He never had to go off, like so many others, to his job. He never needed to have one.

Marriage and beyond

Now that he was financially sound, Michael turned his mind to Nannie Brown once more. He had continued to correspond with her but it was not until 1898 that they actually met again. He knew that Nannie would find coming from a cosmopolitan city like Philadelphia to rural county Kerry well nigh impossible to contemplate. So he took matters into his own hands and set sail for America. He met members of the Brown family and was able to reassure them that he was about to make a settlement with his mother. There was another difficulty though. Nannie had, despite her romance by correspondence, agreed to marry another young man, a New York banker. So Michael knew what he had to do and immediately upon arrival in the Brown household, proposed to Nannie. He asked her to consider her reply as he hurried back home to firm up his financial arrangements with his mother.

On 15 April 1899 Nannie Brown and Michael Rahilly were married in New York. They honeymooned in Europe by taking the Grand Tour. And it was a very long Grand Tour. They visited places in Italy and France and enjoyed all that Europe had to offer. They finally returned to Ireland after months of leisure time. The idea was to meet Michael's family in Ireland. Nannie realised that it was important to make a good impression with Nell and Anna and, most of all, with Ellen Rahilly. She passed her introductions with flying colours and was particularly loved by both of Michael's sisters. They remained firm friends throughout their lives.

The young couple's joy was crowned when their first son, Bobby, was born on 14 March 1900 back in America, although Nannie was quite ill after the delivery. She soon recovered however and they remained in America for some time. Michael came back to Ireland for a visit in the summer of 1900 before going back across the Atlantic to help the Brown family firm whose mills were in the doldrums. Michael did his best to turn around their fortunes but, despite his hard work and enthusiasm, unfortunately the business declined.

Nannie realised that her husband had done all he could to help their ailing business in America and understood Michael's desire to return to his native land. The young family consequently sailed back to Ireland in 1902 where they stayed for a while with his mother at Quinsborough before taking a house in Bray. They lived comfortably with Michael able to indulge his mechanical passion with the purchase of a car and a motorcycle. During 1903 Michael was appointed as a JP just like his father before him. This was probably at the instigation of his mother, as he really had no desire to undertake the duties associated with the honour. He resigned in 1907 for by this time, and probably for some time previously, he had started to show some evidence of anti-British feelings.

But the twists and turns of the lives of Michael and Nannie kept revealing themselves. In June 1903, young Bobby, then aged just 3, developed a fever and suddenly died. Nannie was pregnant at the time and a month later their second son, Richard McEllistrim, was born. This child was always known as 'Mac' and was much loved especially after being born so soon after the death of Bobby. Nannie, having settled reasonably well in Ireland, now took an instant dislike, and even hatred, for the country of her adoption. They were soon out of their Bray house and living for a time in Paris before moving to a house in Brighton on the south coast of England. It was there, on 22 September 1904, that their next son, Aodogan, was born.

Politics enter the frame

Until these early years of the twentieth century politics had really played but a small part in the life of Michael Rahilly. With his privileged upbringing in rural county Kerry he might even have been described as an Irishman with friendly links to the British establishment. He was, as already noted, a Justice of the Peace right up to 1907. He was keen on the Irish language but this was not a particularly prominent nationalist trait. Many western Irish people also spoke it, most as their first tongue. But, by the time he came to live in Brighton, a certain sea change had taken place. His Irish heritage began to take a prime position in his life. It might even have been the very fact that he was now living outside Ireland that he now felt the strong draw of his Irishness.

In 1904 he joined the London branch of the United Irish League which was, to all intents and purposes, the Irish Parliamentary Party now led by John Redmond after the divisive days for the party in the last decade of the nineteenth century following the death of Charles Stewart Parnell. There was never any difficulty in having to take time to travel to the capital for he had no requirement to go to work. At the meetings in London he got to know the Irish MPs including James O'Mara who had been at Clongowes with him. He was regular in his attendance at meetings and he began to advocate the non-attendance of the Irish members at Westminster whilst they had no parliament of their own in Dublin. But he found a certain reticence amongst the MPs and he left the United Irish League in 1905. He had dipped his toes in the parliamentary system and did not much care for it. His ideas on an outright severance from Britain were quickly forming.

Michael became restless living in England and wanted to return to Ireland. He knew Nannie's thoughts on living there again but, in the end, she relented and the family moved into a rented house in Dublin. But 1905 was to bring yet more sadness to the family. Michael's mother, Ellen, died aged just 60 and soon afterwards Nell's husband, David Humphries, also died at a very early age. Hardly had they got over these tragedies when Nannie was summoned back to America to attend a family crisis meeting concerning the future of the Brown family milling business. Things were not going well and Michael was once again asked to try to revive the fortunes of the company. This meant further upheaval when they were required to go back to America so soon after their return to Ireland. They settled back in Philadelphia and Michael set about trying to do what he could to save the business. In the end his endeavours were not successful and they returned to Dublin in 1909 with yet another son, Niall, who had been born in December 1906. Michael was delighted to have come back to the land of his birth at long last. He hoped there would be no further interruptions to prevent him immersing himself in Ireland's struggles against the British.

Whilst he had been in America Michael revived his interest in the Irish language and attended classes there. He regularly kept in touch with what was happening back home and now looked forward to channelling all his energies into an Ireland free from the British yoke.

Having done his duty in America as a devoted son-in-law Michael and his family took up residence in Dublin once more. For a time they rented again and lived close to the home of his sister, Nell, who had been living there since coming up to Dublin from Quinsborough House. But it was not long until they bought 40 Herbert Park in the Ballsbridge suburb and this was to be their home for the remainder of Michael's life. Michael was happy to be back in Ireland and could concentrate on his various interests concerning the future of the country. He started to mix in political circles and there met Arthur Griffith, who had founded Sinn Fein back in 1905. They got on well and Griffith encouraged Michael to help him launch a newspaper, *Sinn Fein Weekly*. Michael was in his element for he was an accomplished writer and journalist. He wrote lots of the articles for the paper himself and went about pressing others to contribute. But like all such papers and broadsheets, finance, or rather the lack of it, was the chief problem. Being in a position to move around at a moment's notice, he sailed for America in an effort to raise funds for the publication. He travelled with William Bulfin whose family was as committed to the cause as the Rahillys. Bulfin had left Ireland in his youth and made his money in Argentina. However the trip was unsuccessful. The pair could make no impression on the Americans despite the large numbers of the diaspora living there. They were disappointed at failing to garner any funds and returned to Dublin with their tails between their legs. The *Sinn Fein Weekly* from January 1910 was no more, having ceased publication. Michael had, nonetheless, gained much experience from his involvement with the paper and Griffith. He was becoming a 'must know' personality in the city.

Life aside from politics

Michael Rahilly's mind was always active and his interests were not exclusively political. Like his father he was interested in inventions. He tried unsuccessfully to get involved with a turf-making machine which would have been of great value to a country like Ireland. He also showed an interest in level crossing barriers which must have been exercising the minds of the safety boffins in the Irish railway system with a view to reducing accidents where the lines crossed the public roads. Nothing came of these inventions, at least as far as Michael Rahilly was concerned, but it clearly demonstrates the kind of fertile brain he had. He even cultivated a friendship with the famous county Down inventor, Harry Ferguson, and they once met on the beach in Newcastle under the mountains of Mourne where Ferguson showed off his fragile aeroplane which, although not exactly a technical success, did at least give Michael and the residents and holiday makers on the county Down coast some fun watching the little aircraft make attempts to get into the air. Ferguson was the inventor here but Michael Rahilly had his sights set on trying to emulate the efforts of Harry Ferguson. Nothing further came of this either but he had, nevertheless, been part of what was to become the flying revolution throughout the early years of the twentieth century.

In November 1911 yet another son, Myles, was born. He had now a little family of four surviving sons. He and Nannie were a contented family unit and, most importantly, Nannie seemed, at long last, to be settled in Ireland. By this year Michael started to call himself The O'Rahilly, emphasising his position as head of the clan and immersing himself totally into Irish culture. His enthusiasm for the language continued unabated even to the extent of a kind of pidgin Irish being regularly spoken at their home in Herbert Park. The family also built a cottage at Ventry in the county

Kerry Gaeltacht where they were able to spend time and speak the language with those whose only language it was.

The Gaelic League now took up much of Michael's time. He, of course, knew the founder, Douglas Hyde, and he threw himself into the efforts of the League, not only to further the language but also to raise funds for their activities. Michael introduced flag days to encourage people to donate and this was probably the first time that this type of fundraising was used in all of Ireland. Flag days became an integral part of Gaelic League open days and competitions. The name of the energetic The O'Rahilly became a household name. Soon he was fighting for the right for the Irish language to be used when addressing letters, when writing cheques and in street names. He met a lot of opposition from the Dublin Castle establishment but, in the end, the government had to concede. He even was practical enough to get Irish script simplified to make it easier to read and to write. He was always dabbling in heraldry and coats of arms as well, to the extent that he started to sell coats of arms to those interested in buying them from him. His enthusiasm was boundless, a fact acknowledged by members of his own family and by those ensconced in all things Irish.

He formed the Irish Topographical Society and spent two years with a great many volunteers in copying valuable Ordnance Survey material which had been locked away in a building in Phoenix Park. For weeks on end, groups of conscientious and dedicated people, The O'Rahilly included of course, walked out from the city centre to undertake what must have been the most boring job imaginable. Yet they saw Michael's vision and supported him. At length the task was completed which, to this day, represents a job well done.

The new king, Edward VII, was due to visit Dublin following his coronation. Normally Ireland would have welcomed the incoming monarch with congratulatory speeches and addresses. But this time the Dublin Corporation had voted not to present the King with such a humble address and The O'Rahilly's pressure on various nationalist groups led to this decision being taken. He organised the populace to protest against the visit and he brought together all the like-minded clubs into a 'United Nationalist Societies' grouping. The King's call on Dublin did go ahead with many citizens supporting him although there was necessarily some ill feeling.

In 1912, the third Home Rule Bill was passed. It would almost certainly become law within two years following the passing of the Parliament Act which broke the stranglehold of the Conservative dominated House of Lords only allowing them to delay legislation by two years at the most. Therefore Home Rule would be enacted by 1914. The O'Rahilly did not like the new Bill for it only gave Dublin very limited powers. By now he was of a firm mind that Irishmen, to become free from Britain, should carry arms. He watched the loyal north arm themselves after the Larne gun running in April 1914. If the unionists would dare to do it then so could and should the southern nationalists.

The Volunteers

Nationalists in the south looked agog at the defiance of the so-called loyalist unionists under Edward Carson. The Ulster Volunteers now numbered some 100,000 men many of whom were already armed. The O'Rahilly demanded that the southerners should do the same. By now the Gaelic League had appointed The O'Rahilly to the post of manager of their publication *The Sword of Light*. This post was ideal for such a man as Michael and he set about encouraging, and then insisting, that anonymous articles professing the more and more physical force nationalist ideas should be signed by their authors. He saw it as cowardice to write leading articles condemning the establishment and not having the determination and guts to sign their names to their articles. This strategy worked and the population could now read the words of people whose names were becoming all the more well known. He got his friend, the scholarly Eoin MacNeill, to approach the leader of the Irish Parliamentary Party, John Redmond, to set up a group of Volunteers in the south similar to those in the north. He then asked MacNeill to become the leader of these Volunteers. The initiative, therefore, for the formation of southern Volunteers was The O'Rahilly's.

The O'Rahilly then further stoked the fire by encouraging Patrick Pearse, who ran his St Enda's school at Rathfarnham, and MacNeill to write some vigorous pieces for *The Sword of Light*. This done to his satisfaction he then proceeded to send out invitations to the first public meeting of the prospective Volunteers at the Rotunda on 25 November 1913. Many other luminaries on the nationalist side claimed that they had initiated the Volunteers, people like Bulmer Hobson, the northern Quaker firebrand, as well as other members of the Irish Republican Brotherhood. But it has since been unequivocally agreed that it was The O'Rahilly's idea. Like all such organisations there were disputes, not least those surrounding the number of members to be part of the senior executive. It ended up with an unwieldy 25 on the committee which of course struggled to agree on anything. However thousands flocked to join from all over the country, initially in the Dublin area. The O'Rahilly was a popular platform speaker and he revelled in his celebrity. At the outset he had always called for three cheers for Edward Carson who had courted notoriety from the British government after setting up the Ulster Volunteers. However this enthusiasm for Carson's actions proved somewhat unpopular with the crowds as the time went on and so Michael took the hint and quietly omitted any reference to the Ulster leader from then on.

The obvious success in recruitment to the Volunteers began to spook Redmond as well as the Dublin Castle authorities. Redmond, whose Irish Parliamentary Party still commanded a great deal of support, now insisted that he nominate committee members for the new movement. He demanded that 25 of his nominees join the 25 already on the clearly unmanageable executive. Redmond got his way but MacNeill and his own group, which included The O'Rahilly, were not disposed to trying to make this huge number work. And so it was that the split came in the new Volunteers. The total involved now numbered over 170,000 but soon MacNeill had siphoned off around 12,000 of this number leaving the rest with Redmond. MacNeill's group retained the Irish Volunteers name whilst Redmond called his the National Volunteers.

The O'Rahilly, whose primary determination was to have his volunteers armed, soon found himself accepting the responsibility of finding weapons and ammunition. This was to prove a formidable task but he, as could have been expected, rose to the occasion. The problems facing him were legion, the first being the collection of money to pay for the arms. He wrote in high hopes to John Devoy in America. Devoy was the much-respected Irish American who had helped Ireland in the past. The O'Rahilly, however, was to be disappointed at Devoy's apparent lack of interest and commitment to the Volunteers. Although Devoy did send $5,000 to assist his cause it did seem a less than adequate response to the urgent need to purchase weapons. The O'Rahilly had, therefore, to look elsewhere for help. He found it in the guise of two Anglo-Irish personalities. Mary Spring Rice and Erskine Childers came to his aid. Both were decidedly generous in financial support and it was Childers who finally agreed to put his yacht *Asgard* at The O'Rahilly's disposal to sail to Germany to bring back the guns and ammunition. Very few of the Irish Volunteers knew of the plan to smuggle the weapons into Ireland apart from MacNeill, Hobson and Sir Roger Casement whose sudden espousal of the Irish nationalist cause was to become legendary.

Childers, after considerable difficulty in purchasing 1,500 guns and associated ammunition, brought 900 of them into Howth harbour north of Dublin on 26 July 1914. The remaining 600 were sailed into Kilcoole in county Wicklow a week later. The O'Rahilly and his celebrated De Dion Bouton motorcar were waiting at Howth and he brought some of the haul into Dublin that day. The day entered Irish nationalist folklore, not just because of the landing of arms, but just as significantly for the so-called Bachelor's Walk 'massacre' when British soldiers shot into the crowds who were watching the arrival of the guns in Dublin city centre. Three people were killed and over thirty injured in the incident. The citizens were incensed and by the end of the week, the numbers of the Volunteers had doubled, most of course associating themselves with the Redmond National Volunteers. Then, a few days later, World War One broke out to further muddy the waters for O'Rahilly and his friends.

As The O'Rahilly was continuing to purchase more weapons, and he had had some success in obtaining a large consignment of Martini Enfield rifles from Birmingham, the volatile situation in Ireland carried on apace. John Redmond, in a speech that was virtually to sign his death warrant, encouraged the Volunteers at an impromptu gathering at Woodenbridge, county Wicklow, to join up and fight for the Allies. Many young men did, of course, follow his exhortation but nationalist Ireland abhorred what the IPP leader had said. Many could simply not believe it, yet over 90% of the volunteers did follow his example. The O'Rahilly and MacNeill strode off with their 10% to pursue their goal. They could finally be rid of Redmond's enforced members on the executive of the Volunteers. They watched helplessly as thousands of young Irishmen were slaughtered in the muddy fields of France and, although most Irish people would not have supported the Germans in the conflict, there certainly was a time when The O'Rahilly did hope that they would win and would then free Ireland from its oppressor. The war was not going well for the British. The appearance of Sir Roger Casement and his abortive recruitment campaign to attract prisoner of war Irishmen to join an Irish brigade only made the situation more difficult in Ireland for the Volunteers and their hierarchy. By 1916 the fact that there was a military council within the ranks of the Volunteers became known to The O'Rahilly. It is reputed that Patrick Pearse even asked him to become a member of this inner sanctum but he declined the offer since he was not a member of the Irish Republican Brotherhood, which was a secret society. Throughout his life he had spoken out against oath bound societies and would never have supported them.

Whatever he did for his various causes The O'Rahilly was always open and transparent about his interest and involvement with them.

The Easter Rising and the death of The O'Rahilly

The O'Rahilly was aware that something was in the air. A rising seemed likely although he was not privy to the plans of the military council. He began to put his affairs in order leaving everything to Nannie. They spent a short holiday some days before Easter when it was discovered that Nannie was expecting yet another child. The O'Rahilly went to see Pearse at St Enda's school to bargain for Bulmer Hobson's release from having been kidnapping by members of Pearse's clique. He was unsuccessful in his endeavours and returned home realising that something seemed imminent. The events of Holy Week 1916 are firmly on record. By the Thursday evening of that week came the impassioned visit by MacNeill to Pearse when he had heard rumours of a rebellion. Pearse admitted that his fears were justified and that the Rising was scheduled for Easter Day. Despite the quandary he was in, MacNeill eventually countermanded Pearse's orders for 'manoeuvres' on Easter Sunday. The O'Rahilly was himself in a dilemma too. It seems that he was, in fact, considering following Pearse and it has even been suggested that he become one of the signatories of the Proclamation. In the end The O'Rahilly stood by the side of MacNeill and was ordered to take the countermanding orders to Limerick on the Sunday. He carried out his duties and delivered the orders, travelling to the west by taxi and not in his De Dion Bouton car.

On the Easter Monday morning the Rising did break out. Pearse and his colleagues knew that they had no option but to proceed. Desmond Fitzgerald arrived at The O'Rahilly's home to tell him what was happening and he immediately donned his uniform and joined the insurgents. He drove down to Liberty Hall to join Pearse and those chosen to approach and take the General Post Office. He was thus one of the first to enter the Post Office as an ADC to Patrick Pearse. He also captured the switch room in the building not long after it had been the stormed. His nephew, Dick Humphries, who was barely 20 years old, was with The O'Rahilly. Nell, the boy's mother and The O'Rahilly's sister, visited the GPO on the Tuesday and convinced her son to go home. He obeyed his mother but was back in the GPO on the Wednesday.

During the days in the General Post Office The O'Rahilly looked after the dozen or so prisoners they had captured. These were young members of the forces and the police who just happened to be in the building at the time when it was taken over. The prisoners were full of praise for The O'Rahilly who always made sure that they were properly fed and looked after. As the battle raged the GPO was reduced to a burning ruin by the Friday. Pearse ordered The O'Rahilly to gather twelve men to get out of the Post Office and capture the nearby Moore Street barracks. By late evening on the Friday The O'Rahilly had his men briefed and they made their way outside. It was not long before the small party was shot upon by British soldiers in the area. The O'Rahilly was shot not long afterwards and died there some hours later. He had time to write a note to his wife and children and this note was discovered by a soldier who had the decency to deliver the letter to Nannie at Herbert Park. He had died a martyr's death in a Rising that he may have wanted but which he had not totally approved of. As was said, or so it is reputed, 'he had helped to wind the clock, then he should be there when it struck'. He was buried in a temporary grave at Glasnevin not long after the events and was reinterred the following year in the Republican plot. Thus ended the life of an Irishman whose whole existence had been centred on an Ireland free from the British yoke. He did not, however, live to see it.

Suggested reading
1. Bourke, Marcus, *The O'Rahilly*, Tralee, 1965.
2. O'Rahilly, Aodogan, *Winding the Clock – O'Rahilly and the 1916 Rising*, Dublin, 1991.

Hugh Lane

Enterprising and eclectic – art lover and
flamboyant dandy

The early years of an extraordinary man

During the latter half of the nineteenth century art and culture at long last began once again to blossom in Ireland. It was the time when Irish song, Irish games, Irish literature and the Irish language began to show their worth. In the field of painting Ireland did have a number of well-known artists like Sarah Purser, Walter Osborne and John B. Yeats. In the midst of this burgeoning revival there was born on 9 November 1875, at Ballybrack House in the wealthy suburb of Douglas in the city of Cork, a boy christened Hugh Percy, the son of Adelaide and James Lane. He was to be one of a relatively large family of his impecunious Anglican clergyman father and his high born titled mother.

Adelaide Persse was one of sixteen children of Dudley Persse, a member of the Anglo-Irish aristocracy whose stately home was Roxborough near Loughrea in county Galway. The Persses were unimpressed by Adelaide's choice of husband and frowned upon the proposed union. They did everything they could to prevent the marriage, but to no avail. In the end the young couple married but, from the outset and despite the number of children born, it was a most unhappy and miserable marriage. Although Hugh was born in Ireland, the family soon moved to Bath where James Lane was appointed to a curacy in a local Church of England parish there. By 1877 he had become the vicar of Redruth in Cornwall. The thoughts of moving to this lovely county soon dissipated. Redruth was in the middle of the copper mining area of Cornwall and the whole place was most depressing and very ugly. This only added to the unhappiness within the Lane marriage and it was not long before Adelaide took off with her children to live in different parts of England leading the life of an itinerant. She was supported financially by her own parents who, in some ways, must have approved of their daughter's newfound travelling lifestyle. At least she was apart from her unloving husband who got on with his task of caring for his hardworking parishioners. Adelaide eventually returned to the Redruth rectory but she never performed the duties of a vicar's wife nor, for that matter, those of a typical housewife. The Lanes finally separated in 1893 never to see one another again.

As a consequence of their nomadic lifestyle the Lane children never received any regular education. In later life they just about managed although few of them, apart from Ruth, lived much beyond forty years of age. Hugh, like his siblings, suffered from his patchy education, something which rather unfavourably affected him throughout his life. His health, too, often caused concern and he went through childhood as a sickly and fragile child. He did, on the positive side however, spend his summer holidays at Roxborough with his grandparents and the throng of young Persse cousins. Amidst this extensive clan there stood out one aunt who was to become one of his greatest supporters and one to whom Hugh could, and did, often turn for help. This was his aunt Augusta who became Lady Gregory in 1880. She herself, of course, went on to leave her indelible mark on Ireland in the early days of the twentieth century with her legacy of the foundation of the Abbey Theatre in Dublin.

Making his way in the world

By his late teenage years Hugh wanted to be away from home, such as it was, so he turned to his aunt Augusta for help and advice. It was readily given and the job, which his dear aunt found for him, was to lead him into a world of art collectors and connoisseurs of fine paintings and sculptures. He settled himself into the central London gallery of Martin Colnaghi, one of the best-known dealers in the metropolis. Hugh became his assistant at the princely salary of £1 per week. Colnaghi may not have been the best and most caring employer but he certainly taught Hugh Lane all he knew about this up and coming profession.

The last decade of the nineteenth century was an ideal time to be in the art dealing business. Many of the country's finest paintings of the old masters were becoming available. Many of the landed gentry were becoming financially strapped and were happy to sell their fine paintings and portraits to realise much needed income. As it happened it was even a more difficult time for Irish landowners as they were not only receiving smaller rentals from their tenants than their English counterparts but, because of the exertions of the Land Leaguers, were often not even being paid any rent at all. Money was urgently required to pay their own overheads and so works of art, which had been in the possession of many of the families for centuries, were simply taken off the walls of their great mansions and sold to art dealers.

Hugh Lane immediately saw the potential in the profession into which he had been catapulted. He and Colnaghi soon parted company which presented no problem at all for young Lane. He already had customers of his own and he had the happy knack of attracting business from the wealthy landowners, both in England and in Ireland. He knew how to cultivate friendships which meant that he was the first port of call for many of the great landlords. He was barely twenty years of age and yet he had all sorts of rich clientele. One of these was Lord Fermoy who was happy to sell many of his great works to the young and relatively inexperienced Lane. Hugh was also astute enough to look around and learn from those men in the art dealing business who were soon to become his rivals. He also saw many of the country's greatest masterpieces being sold outside the British Isles and going to dealers in America and South Africa. And he had to be careful to resist the temptation of becoming, like so many others, an unscrupulous dealer. Many in his profession had gained the reputation of offering ridiculously low prices for art works of the highest merit and then selling them for outrageous profits. For his entire life Hugh Lane stood firm and gave fair prices for what he bought. And yet he did become a very wealthy man.

Starting a business of his own

Hugh Lane moved on and went into partnership with E.T. Turner at the Carlton Gallery in London. However this venture did not work out and Lane had even to go to the law to recoup his salary. He won his case but the experience left a bad taste in his mouth. From now on he would be his own boss. And so he set up his own small gallery in Pall Mall from where he built up a lucrative business and an enviable reputation. He became a 'one man band' working entirely on his own without even ever hiring a secretary. He not only bought and sold at his gallery and made visits to the homes of prospective clients, he even wrote all his own correspondence. He was the archetypal lone dealer but he was soon considered by those in his own profession to be perhaps the most successful dealer in town. He may not have had much formal education but he had an eye that could spot a painting of great worth and then buy it for a reasonable price. He bought, in his earliest days, a Gainsborough for a couple of hundred pounds and then made a handsome profit on it. Art dealing doubtless was a true vocation but within its ranks were many shady characters who engaged in illegal practices. There were many forgeries and misattributions and profits were regularly made at the expense of trusting vendors. Hugh Lane steered clear of these disreputable people as best he could. He had made a wise decision to go it alone.

The successful businessman

Lane's career quickly flourished. Within the first year of setting up his own gallery, he had already made a great deal of money from buying inexpensively and selling on at a decent profit. One of his particular skills was being able to spot a valuable picture which was dirty and had been badly cared for. He often bought those unkempt portraits and set about cleaning them. In his earlier days he had acquired this expertise and it was to stand him in good stead throughout his career. He had the patience to bring a magnificent canvas back to life. Many of his rivals were plainly jealous of Lane's abilities and, when he bought a Rembrandt for £1,000 and a Velasquez for just £200, the art dealing world realised they had a formidable opponent in the purchasing stakes. Hugh Lane may only have been in the business for a year or two but he was already a very wealthy man, earning upwards of £10,000 in a year. This in the late 1890s was an incredible income and Hugh Lane used it to best advantage as he bought and sold masterpieces at breathtaking speed.

But there was one anomaly in Hugh Lane's makeup. He may have spent hundreds of pounds in the morning buying a painting of great worth, yet he continued to live in cramped rented accommodation. And, stranger still, he refused to feed himself properly. Rather than visiting the fine restaurants in central London where he worked, he had the infuriating habit of going into the dingiest corner shops to buy little more than scraps of food. He would sit down in his gallery with perhaps a sandwich and a cup of tea and this frugal fare would do him for the rest of the day. And what was the reason? It was probably because he had no one at his side to watch over and take care of him.

Thus was Hugh Lane quite the enigma. He may have been wealthy but he continued to be penny-pinching in his eating habits. However when it came to dressing Hugh Lane was an altogether different man. Tall at 6', and spare with a high-pitched voice and a somewhat effeminate appearance, he loved to spend money on good clothes for he determined to be the immaculate gentleman. He was, in fact, the archetypal dandy. Apart from playing the piano occasionally, he had no hobbies or pastimes apart from his work. Neither had he many close friends. Over the years he cultivated the friendship of a number of protégés, mainly young men who showed an interest in Lane and his business. He also loved arranging tea parties to which he would invite titled and genteel ladies. He would, in return, be invited to many of the classy salons in the city of London and would enjoy the attention shown to him as one of London's leading art experts. Whilst in these wonderful and extravagant stately apartments, Lane would often re-arrange ornaments and other objets d'art to fit in with his taste and to show off his particular expertise. Most of the grandes dames would tolerate, and even appreciate, Lane's quirks, whilst others would simply replace their items when he had left.

By the age of 25, Hugh Lane finally moved into much more prestigious accommodation in more comfortable chambers in fashionable Jermyn Street. He spent his time and money decorating his new home and enjoyed bringing his acquaintances to tea parties there. By this stage in his life, he had few contacts left with his family. He saw his mother occasionally but their relationship somewhat soured as the years went by. None of his brothers did well and even his eldest brother, Alfred, was only remembered as having been mauled to death by a pack of lions in South Africa. His father remained in deepest Cornwall ministering to the spiritual needs of his flock there. His closest family contact was with his younger sister, Ruth, who became more and more a part of his life as the years rolled by. His nearest and dearest relative, however, continued to be his aunt Augusta Gregory and he spent time at Coole Park in county Galway as often as he could, enjoying her company and that of his cousin, Robert Gregory. However Hugh Lane was never very popular with the other regular visitors to Coole Park, the aesthetes W. B. Yeats, George Russell and Douglas Hyde. Lane was too dapper and sophisticated to fit in, although little did he care.

Hugh Lane looks to Ireland

As his wealth and reputation increased so did Hugh Lane continue on his successful quests to buy and sell marvellous works of art. He made regular visits abroad, calling at the finest galleries on the continent of Europe. Although considered a man of standing throughout France and Italy, he never really warmed to the locals. He preferred his own company as he sought out those elusive paintings and sculptures.

But then, on his visits back to Ireland, he found himself amidst the great and the good there and was soon a habitué amongst the so-called Castle set. These were the people who attended the various stylish events at Dublin Castle with the Viceroy and his friends.

Hugh Lane was now in his element as he cultivated a close circle of friends with titles. He particularly liked consorting with Lord and Lady Drogheda and Lord and Lady Mayo who were very much involved in the arts, and who owned many precious paintings. More and more Hugh Lane began to revel in his newfound company. He got to know the enigmatic Sarah Purser who was not only a talented portraitist herself but was also the great mixer and fixer in the Dublin art world. She was always encouraging Irish artists to exhibit their work and had, for example, recently promoted a show of the paintings of John B. Yeats and Nathaniel Hone. Lane admired Miss Purser's determination and drive but he also saw that he himself could become a patron of the Irish arts. He bought pieces by both Yeats and Hone and he started to encourage other younger artists like William Orpen, Augustus John and Gerald Kelly. He felt he had found his niche. He would now expend his money and his energies on the promotion of Ireland's native painters. In many ways he had discovered his vocation. Although he was, from now on, to continue to live in London, Hugh Lane's main energies were to become focussed on Dublin and the Irish art scene there.

Too many of Ireland's young artists, however, were leaving Ireland to live and work in England and further afield. John Lavery was the prime example of a brilliant young painter and, as such, one whom the country could ill afford to lose. The Royal Hibernian Academy, which had been founded in 1823, was very much in the doldrums and, although it still held its regular annual exhibitions, it was failing to attract either the right kind of exhibitor or even the crowds to view their works on show. And to add to their woes, their gallery was in a most unfashionable locale in Lower Abbey Street. Something needed to be done, and urgently. Hugh Lane entered the breach and prevailed upon the academicians to allow him to mount an exhibition of old masters. Why they were so reluctant was a mystery for it was clear that to promote such a worthwhile showing would bring prestige at last to this noble institution. In the end they relented and Lane set about finding and borrowing works of art to put on display. His timescale was short but he was successful not only in showing works never seen before but also in proving what an asset Dublin could have in having Lane on their side. The exhibition was a great success and many glowing reports found their way into the daily newspapers not just in Dublin but also in London and on the continent. A great many visitors paid their entrance fees to see the works on show which gave the Academy just the boost it needed as well as funds to swell its depleted coffers. Like all successes, of course, there were detractors and the one problem, which slightly tainted the success of the venture, was a dispute over Lane's attribution of a Reynolds painting. Lane usually was correct in his attributions over such matters although on this occasion he may have been wrong. But this hardly mattered as the exhibition had brought the Academy once again to prominence.

Lane was generally praised for his work in bringing together works of art for the public to admire. This, in many ways, was his raison d'être. But he was first and foremost an art dealer which meant that if he could purchase some of the paintings on display, then he would do so. It was his job; he had a living to make. Many of his detractors accused him of taking advantage of the plethora of Irish landlords and members of the gentry who had offered to show their works of art. They saw Lane as making a killing when he saw paintings he wanted and then buying them at knock down prices. He simply shrugged off this criticism and, for the most part, the owners of the works he bought seemed happy enough with the prices offered by Lane.

More exhibitions

The grandees of the Royal Hibernian Academy had a rather schizophrenic view of Hugh Lane. There was no doubt that he had brought their annual exhibition into the limelight once again after many years of disappointing gate receipts. When they decided to mount a posthumous show for Walter Osborne who had died young aged 43 in 1903, the academicians ignored Hugh Lane. They ran the show themselves. Lane simply got on with his work and ignored the Academy's snub.

But in 1904 another opportunity came for the flamboyant Lane to shine. The World Fair was being held in St Louis in the United States and Lane felt this was the time for Ireland to send a fine selection of works where they would be seen by the great and the good of the art world. So he set about his task of collecting and borrowing paintings with a purpose. He visited his titled friends and encouraged them to lend their masterpieces. Some, however, were reluctant to send their priceless works so far away but most succumbed to Hugh Lane's dynamism and persuasive powers. But, in the end, the Irish works were not sent across the Atlantic. The insurance premiums proved exorbitant and so the Irish works stayed at home in Ireland. Another of Lane's ventures had hit the buffers but he was not to be outdone. The exhibits he had assembled, over 450 of them, were packed up and sent to London where they were shown to large crowds to rave reviews.

In the final months of 1904 Lane mounted yet another exhibition at the Royal Hibernian Academy. When those staid and sedate academicians heard Lane's latest proposal they could hardly believe their ears. Lane had been able to obtain permission to show 160 of the top ranking paintings which had belonged to the late wealthy Scottish engineering magnate, James Staats Forbes. In his lifetime Forbes had accumulated no less than 4,000 priceless works of art and was probably the greatest collector of art works of his generation. The show, however, only met with mixed reviews and was not altogether a success. Lane was able to buy a number of the works but had he been given more support from the Academy he might have been in a position to make more purchases for them. Lane's tenacity did not falter and he moved on to his next project.

Hugh Lane's preference in paintings was for the old masters and he had collected many well known works in this genre. But the early years of the twentieth century were now dominated by the Impressionists. Lane did not care for these modern works although, shrewd businessman that he was, he still ensured that he bought whatever paintings became available, regardless of style. He purchased works by, for example, Corot and Manet, and pursued others when he had customers for them. But he remained throughout his life a lover and connoisseur of Gainsborough and his fellow old masters.

Hugh Lane decides on Ireland

Hugh Lane turned 30 in 1905, already a very wealthy man. He was also a very committed man as could clearly be seen in his advocacy of Irish painters and his enthusiasm for showing the Irish public popular works of art. By this relatively early age he had also, of necessity, drawn up his will. He had originally wanted to leave his art works to the National Gallery in London. This seemed natural and sensible for he did live there after all. But, despite setbacks with the old academicians in Dublin, he now made up his mind that his works should not go to London but to Dublin. He had seen the pleasure that the recent shows had given to the ordinary people of Dublin and he determined that the city's gallery should be moved out of Lower Abbey Street and its dismal surroundings to a new municipal gallery in a more salubrious and appropriate venue. This seemed a wise course; it made a great deal of sense; it was worthy of support. This became Hugh Lane's life work. Little did he know it, but it was to become the life work of many art enthusiasts in Dublin for generations to come, even until the present day at the beginning of the twenty first century.

He now set about finding donors to fill such a gallery. He did, of course, continue to buy works for the venture himself but he was able to encourage such artists as Constance and Casimir Markievicz to donate works that they had recently completed. The Royal Hibernian academicians were largely supportive of Lane's enthusiastic idea although there were detractors. But the Academy saw that, for the first time in years, gifts of paintings began flowing in. The new gallery, when it came, would now have an enviable collection to adorn its walls. Like everything that Lane was involved in, it led to lots of media coverage. The newspapers were full of the latest ideas from Hugh Lane and the public was clearly getting in behind the project. Lane even got his sister, Ruth, to make albums of all the paper clippings which, in due course, increased to many volumes. There were public meetings held to promote the new gallery and at one of them the new Viceroy, Lord Aberdeen, was in attendance. This show of such influential support augured well for the future.

Hugh Lane, whose plans were supported by Dublin Corporation, promised to donate art works himself and continued to encourage donations from the public. But delays in pursuing the project soon took the edge off Lane's enthusiasm. While Dublin was procrastinating Lane decided to bring the exhibits he already owned to the new gallery to Belfast where a successful show was mounted.

In the midst of all this planning a collection was being made by friends of Lane to pay for a portrait of himself by the artist, John Sargent. Hugh Lane particularly liked this artist and was very pleased with the outcome. It remained one of Lane's most precious possessions. Not long afterwards Lane had his Italian artist friend, Antonio Mancini, execute another portrait of himself. This large painting showed the true Hugh Lane; nervous, uncomfortable and ill at ease.

The question of whether or not he would now buy a house in Dublin became paramount. His aunt Augusta told him that she thought it was essential that he had an Irish domicile; his friends and gallery supporters added their encouragement; even members of the public expressed their desire to see such a fine man come to live in their midst. Whilst Lane dithered about making up his mind, those who were critical of Hugh Lane made their views known. Many looked on him with suspicion advocating that Lane was only showing an interest in Irish art for his own financial gain. He was, true enough, still mixing with the Castle set and he was forever looking for appointment to an official post. He continued buying great masters himself including a priceless Titian and even a Renoir which he bought in 1907 for £1,600. On balance Hugh Lane, regardless of his drive to have a new gallery for Dublin established, was still a businessman. While he was attracting works for the gallery he was offering his services as an art dealer to those who engaged him. He even engaged artists whose expertise was in copying old masters for impoverished aristocrats who needed to sell their originals but who did not want their family and friends to know that the fine old masters on the walls of their home were now, in fact, just copies. They all had the best of both worlds. The gentry still had their artworks, albeit copied, whilst Lane had often bought the original.

A gallery – of sorts

Lane regularly showed his displeasure at the amount of time it was taking Dublin Corporation to find suitable premises for the new gallery. He continued to harass them until, after a delay of well over a year, a former private residence at 17 Harcourt Street was earmarked for the gallery. It was essentially a stopgap measure although Lane soon set about making it into a worthy exhibition space. He was appointed honorary director, something which greatly pleased him and, by early 1908, the gallery was open. There were over 300 exhibits of which one third were Lane's own private gifts. The opening ceremony was a lavish affair with the house packed full of guests. Lane was publicly thanked for all his hard work and his unfailing generosity. For his efforts Hugh Lane was made an Honorary Freeman of Dublin and elected to the governing body of University College Dublin. The gallery became an immediate success with the ordinary citizens of Dublin which was, after all, the whole idea of having it. They flocked to it in their thousands and were able to gain free entry, another of Lane's wishes for having the place at all. The only down side was the fact that the venture was soon in financial difficulties. This was a matter for the Corporation and a problem never entirely resolved then or afterwards.

A home of his own – but in London

Whilst Lane obviously enjoyed the work he was doing in Dublin and also the close contacts he had with many people in Ireland, including connections with the Abbey theatre, he gravitated once more to London. 1909 was a significant year for him. His mother had died in the February and his father, in some contact in recent years with his son, soon remarried although he himself would die the following year.

In the King's birthday honours, Hugh Lane received a knighthood for services to the art world. He was, of course, pleased with such an accolade, which rather appealed to his vanity and, it has to be said, to his snobbery. He soon bought Lindsey House in Chelsea which was a building of great design and merit. He set about restoring it and making countless fabulous changes. He filled it with old masters and every kind of artwork. His guests to his favourite session of high tea were enraptured with the house. Very often guests would admire a particular objet d'art and he would simply take the item off the mantelpiece or side table, and give it to them. This was a particular trait of Lane's which proved popular with his visitors, naturally enough. Regular callers at Lindsey House included his aunt Augusta and two of London society's grandes dames, the Duchess of Rutland and the Marchioness of Ripon. Hugh Lane always aimed high although another friend and visitor, the Irish artist, Sarah Cecilia Harrison, came from more humble origins.

Hugh Lane had, however, one particular vice and that was gambling. For such a punctilious and driven man it almost seems hard to believe that he would regularly set off for the casino tables at places like Monte Carlo where he squandered and lost very large sums of money. Although he occasionally won a little money and would buy perhaps some jewellery, he often returned to London penniless, sometimes actually having to borrow money for his return fare. This was a side of Sir Hugh Lane which would have surprised lots of his friends and acquaintances. It was, nonetheless, an integral part of his complicated personality.

The South African connection

As a renowned art dealer, Hugh Lane became acquainted with many people who had made their fortunes in gold and diamonds in South Africa. A number of them had spent a great deal of money setting up homes in London and buying country mansions in the Home Counties. These 'nouveaux riches', with plenty of money to spare, then started to acquire old masters, often purchased from impecunious aristocrats and, naturally enough, with the help of the famous Hugh Lane.

Florence and Lionel Phillips were two such randlords. Florence was keen to have a public art gallery for Johannesburg and, having struck up a marvellous rapport with Lane, was encouraged by him to visit the world's most prestigious galleries. But Lane was shrewd enough to get her interested in modern painters rather than in the old masters which were becoming prohibitive in price. Florence succumbed to Lane's charms and was soon buying and receiving donations of paintings and money to adorn the walls of her new gallery. Although the gallery was opened in 1910, the fully restored one did not open until 1915, by which time Lane was dead.

Another wealthy German-born South African, Max Michaelis, now wanted to sponsor a gallery in Cape Town and Lane was engaged to buy as many works for it as he could. Many Dutch masters, like Hals and Rembrandt, were purchased by Lane and sold on to Michaelis. They were exhibited in London before being shipped to Cape Town. The relationship between Michaelis and Lane was strained and Michaelis even accused Lane of duping him, which proved unfounded. This venture was not one of Lane's finest hours and he was pleased to be out of Michaelis's clutches.

Concentrating on England and Ireland once more

Hugh Lane always preferred the old masters but this did not prevent him from buying impressionist and post-impressionist works. He was an astute businessman and he realised that these works were where he could and would make his money. To add to this important factor, these works were less expensive to buy and Lane's intuition as a dealer made him believe that this is where money would now be made. He set up exhibitions in London and Dublin presenting these modern works by such artists as Cézanne and van Gogh. They were not very popular with the public and the critics who considered these painters to be either insane or imposters or both.

All this incessant pressure made Hugh Lane much more irascible and sickly. He had little time for himself and yet, in the midst of this disruption, he became briefly engaged to Lady Clare Annesley whose home was in Castlewellan in county Down. She was only half his age but he never seemed to have his heart in the matter of marriage. Many said that he was, in fact, a homosexual although, once more, there seems little to substantiate this claim. Hugh Lane simply seemed one of those people who truly was in love with his work and never with another human being, female or male. He did have a number of young male protégés, like Thomas Bodkin for example, but these relationships almost certainly proved innocent. His health suffered at this more stressful time and he even agreed to take time out and book himself into a rest home. He was now doubtless very aware of his own mortality. However he was soon back to his frenetic, if less enthusiastic, lifestyle; he felt that whatever time was left to him that he should make the best possible use of it.

That elusive Dublin gallery

Nearly five years had elapsed since the temporary gallery at Harcourt Street had been opened. Numbers visiting it were still impressive and, in fact, the Prime Minister, Herbert Asquith, had made a call in the company of Hugh Lane in July 1912. He had been impressed by the exhibits but had criticised the gallery's location. He expressed his wish that a more suitable location should quickly be found. This view strengthened Lane's stance as he was, by now, entirely incensed by the Dublin Corporation's inaction.

Now, for the first time, Lane threatened to remove the paintings he had loaned if the new gallery did not quickly materialise. On this list of 39 paintings were many precious works of art and he had consistently told the Dublin authorities that he was happy to donate many of them when the new gallery came to fruition. These pictures were considered to be the envy of the world. Many a gallery in the world would have given their all to have such works in their cities. At the same time he was considering who best to design the new premises. His choice fell upon Edward Lutyens, a most talented English architect. A plan was hatched to build a fitting and attractive gallery in St Stephen's Green, but the idea was scuppered by Lord Ardilaun, whose park it was. Lane was more than disappointed and was beginning to think that his gallery would never be built.

There was, however, some success at least in raising funds for the building of the new gallery to add to the meagre amount promised by Dublin Corporation. Suggestion after suggestion for an alternative building was proposed but none to Lane's liking. He approached Lutyens once more who then drew up most ambitious plans for a bridge gallery to be built over the river Liffey in the centre of Dublin. The idea was far-sighted but probably too grand. It would not have suited Dublin and this plan, too, was dropped. The fact that Lutyens was not an Irishman (although his mother was Irish) did not enamour many in Dublin especially when Home Rule and the threat of civil disturbances were in the air. Hugh Lane never seemed sensitive to the current thinking in Dublin and this seeming arrogance counted against him. More and more of the influential people in Dublin were determined to work against Lane in his endeavours to bring a new municipal gallery to Dublin. To many this venture only rated as a low priority. Improving the quality of life for Dublin's slum dwellers seemed more important than spending much needed funds on a luxury such as an art gallery. 1913 with the Great Dublin Lock Out, which affected thousands of Dublin's lowly paid workers, finally ended the battle for the Liffey gallery.

A rebuffed Lane changes his will

For the time being Lane had had enough of the Dublin authorities and, as he saw it, their pettiness. He went to London where he met the directors of the National Gallery who were anxious to exhibit his 39 paintings. Some of them were not front line masterpieces but many of them were well worth having. Hugh Lane took a step too far, or at least it was so to prove for decades following. He willed his pictures to London just to spite Dublin. In his heart of hearts he still wanted them displayed in Ireland but he had suffered too much from the inconsistencies of the Irish. Needless to say London was delighted; what the Dublin people said can only be the subject of conjecture.

Hugh Lane's health, which was always rather delicate, deteriorated in the autumn of 1913 when he was diagnosed as suffering from neurasthenia, a psychological illness with physical manifestations. He tried hypnosis but to no avail. The condition was to trouble him for the remainder of his life. At least he had his lovely home at Lindsey House where he could entertain when he felt in better spirits. And he also had the company of his sister, Ruth, who had recently been widowed and, having no children, was able to come to stay with her brother. The arrangement worked out well for both of them and he could come and go in the sure knowledge that Ruth would care for his house and its valuable possessions.

He made his first visit to America but it proved unsuccessful both from the point of view of not selling many paintings and also because he generally found his American hosts to be somewhat uninformed and uncultured.

Back home in London Lane heard that Sir Walter Armstrong was retiring as Director of the National Gallery of Ireland. He coveted the job and made this fact quite clear by openly canvassing for the position. He was already on the Board but had been irregular in his attendance. Now he stepped up his presence and started to offer yet more precious works to the gallery. This seemed the way of making your mark for a post a century ago and so, after a few scares, Sir Hugh Lane was appointed as the Director.

An official position at last

Lane immediately made changes. Firstly he declined to receive his salary so that the gallery could purchase more pictures. Lane continued to present more valuable works and then set about renovating the building at his own expense. There was no doubting his commitment to the gallery although it still resided in unsatisfactory surroundings. Being the stickler for fashion he was Lane ordered his court uniform as National Director, although none of his predecessors ever had such ceremonial dress. In all likelihood no one probably ever knew that such courtly trappings were ever associated with the post. Once more, of course, Lane did not trouble the gallery's accountants to settle the bill for the uniform. He paid for it himself.

His aunt Augusta was evidently very pleased that her nephew had been appointed to such a prestigious post. She now implored him to buy a house in Dublin. But her entreaties fell on deaf ears and Lane continued to commute to and from London and Dublin for what remained of his life. In fact, when he was back in England, he took up horse riding with a passion and vigour associated with younger and more robust gentlemen. He also bought, and dangerously drove, a motor car. Many must have wondered at Hugh Lane's Damascus road conversion to this hazardous and reckless life style. Sadly he did not live long enough to enjoy much more of this panache and flamboyance.

The final pages are written

By the time the Great War broke out in 1914 life for art dealers, and particularly for Sir Hugh Lane, became precarious. No one was buying or selling works of art and Lane found himself in difficult financial straits. He was in a quandary as to what best to do. Although many of his friends and acquaintances were joining up and going off to war, this was never an option for Lane himself. His health was poor and he would not have been considered fit enough to enlist. As the new year of 1915 dawned, and with no end in sight to the war that was supposed to have been concluded by Christmas 1914, Hugh Lane made another fateful decision. He had agreed to go to America early in 1915 although he was most apprehensive because of U boat attacks on ships sailing across the Atlantic. Before setting out he wrote out a codicil to his will changing his decision to leave his 39 paintings to London and now offering them back to Dublin provided, of course, that a suitable gallery was built to house them within five years. His mind was made up and he packed his bags and sailed from Liverpool to New York. He had, however, omitted one thing. He had not had the codicil witnessed as required by law to make it binding. And he locked the document in a drawer without any instructions to anyone that it even existed.

Hugh Lane completed his business in New York quite quickly and left America on the Lusitania on 1 May 1915. The great liner never made it to its destination. Off the Cork coast and within sight of his birthplace, Hugh Lane, along with hundreds of others aboard ship, was drowned when a torpedo from a German U boat sent the vessel to the bottom of the sea. Hugh Lane's body was never found. The survivors were taken to Cork and other small surrounding ports. The world grieved at such a horrific loss and the art world, and the members of Lane's family, were left wondering what would be his legacy.

A memorial service was held in Chelsea on 20 May and a plaque was erected in St Luke's church in Douglas in the city of Cork. Tributes flowed in to the memory of a man whose contribution to the arts would be long remembered; they would never see his like again; their world would be an emptier place.

The aftermath of the tragedy
Lane's sudden and untimely death left the London and Dublin art worlds reeling. They hardly knew what to do. The directorship of

the National Gallery of Ireland went first to Walter Strickland and then to Robert Langton Douglas. These appointments were not universally popular especially amongst such protégés of Hugh Lane's as Thomas Bodkin. The gallery held on to 42 of Lane's paintings which were there at the time of his death, although it did seem clear that Lane had wanted them sold. But there they remained to form a significant part of the works on show. His estate was sold off but, because of the war and depressed prices, not a great deal of money was realised. What money accrued to the gallery, however, enabled them to buy more works over the subsequent years.

Finding a biographer then proved extremely difficult. Two prospective authors were approached but nothing came of this endeavour. In the end his aunt Lady Augusta Gregory agreed to write the book. This she did to the best of her ability although, to be fair, it tended not to be as objective as it could have been. But the biography did appear in 1921 under the rather cumbersome title of *Hugh Lane's Life and Achievement, with some Account of the Dublin Galleries* and was published by John Murray of London. This volume served as the sole text on Sir Hugh Lane for very many years to come.

But the greatest problem, by far, was the fact that Lane had not had the codicil to his will properly witnessed. It also took some time to find as it had been secreted away in a locked drawer at Lindsey House. When it was eventually discovered, far from bringing relief to the searchers, it brought untold misery and difficulty to his executor, his aunt Lady Gregory. The 39 paintings were in London at the time of Hugh Lane's death. The National Gallery there had accepted the works from Lane but had reneged and only, after much persuasion, agreed to store them in the vaults of the gallery. When Lane died, however, although they had been obviously reluctant to show them, London decided to hold on to them. Dublin objected as it was clear, or so they surmised, that Lane had meant the paintings for them. But the codicil had not been witnessed and so London kept them. Lady Gregory fought tooth and nail to have the pictures returned and even got Michael Collins to bring up the matter at the Treaty talks in late 1921.

For years the saga of the 39 paintings was the subject of correspondence, of debates in the House of Commons and letters to the editor of all the national newspapers in Ireland and in Great Britain. There seemed to be no solution in sight and neither there was. It became Augusta Gregory's sole life aim to have the paintings returned. When she died aged 80 in 1932, there was still no resolution to the dilemma.

By 1933 the municipal gallery in Dublin, after years in unsatisfactory premises in Harcourt Street, moved to a fine town house, Charlemont House, in Merrion Square. Money was spent extending the building and it became a favourite outing for the citizens of Dublin, as was Hugh Lane's original aim. The 39 paintings in London had been, by this time, exhibited in the new extension to the Tate Gallery and there they remained. But, with Lady Gregory's death, the momentum was lost and it was not until 1959 that an agreement was reached to allow Dublin to have half the pictures for five years at a time. In 1979, 30 were permitted to stay in Dublin with the remaining ones being shared over the year.

The whole unwieldy and cumbersome business rumbled on until 2008 when the entire group of paintings was finally exhibited in Dublin for the first time since Hugh Lane's death. This is a story which has held the Irish art world's undivided attention for 100 years. But the clear wish of that most enigmatic man and scholar of beautiful paintings, Sir Hugh Lane, appears, at very long last, to have come to fruition.

Suggested reading

1. Bodkin, Thomas, *Hugh Lane and his Pictures*, Dublin, c. 1934.
2. O'Byrne, Robert, *Hugh Lane – 1875-1915*, Dublin, 2000.

Thomas MacDonagh

Aspirant poet and playwright – a reluctant revolutionary

Early life and education

This future poet, revolutionary and signatory to the Proclamation following the Easter Rising, yet one so often overlooked and forgotten, was born on 1 February 1878 in the village of Cloughjordan in north county Tipperary. Thomas was the fourth child of his parents, but the first to survive infancy. Joseph MacDonagh, a schoolteacher, had married Mary Parker in 1868 and, after the unspeakable sadness of losing their first three children, went on to have six more, three sons and three daughters. In effect, therefore, Thomas became the eldest of their family. The MacDonaghs lived in a modest house in the village which had, at that time, a sizeable protestant community. Catholics worshipped outside Cloughjordan at a little place called Grawn although relations between the communities and the Big House were cordial.

Mary MacDonagh had been brought up as an Anglican but following her marriage she converted to Roman Catholicism and became, like so many other converts, extremely zealous and committed to her new found religion. She was a very intelligent woman who wrote short stories and encouraged all her children to follow suit. Young Thomas was blessed with two such gifted parents and was always greatly influenced by them, particularly by his mother. Early on he did start to write and even attempted an autobiographical novel and some poems by the time of his teenage years. The MacDonaghs were little interested in politics although Ireland was, even then in the 1880s and 1890s, in the grip of Home Rule fever, following the violent actions of the Land Leaguers. In many ways this disinterest in what was going on in the country was rather strange since both parents were so socially conscious and involved in life around them. When Thomas left Cloughjordan, aged 14 in 1892, to continue his education, he rarely returned to his home place and only then during his mother's lifetime.

Thomas was sent to Rockwell College, near Cashel, which had been founded in 1864. It was known as 'the Scotch College' because, for many years, it was the training school for Holy Ghost fathers who would undertake their vocations in Scotland. French was spoken by the staff and students almost as much as English. Throughout his life Thomas was, therefore, most proficient in French, which was to come in useful later when he spent time in Paris. Rockwell was not influenced by the revival of the Irish language, a campaign then being enthusiastically promoted by Douglas Hyde and, from 1893 onwards, by the Gaelic League. Rather than play Gaelic games, the boys of Rockwell were keen on retaining cricket and rugby, the so-called 'garrison' sports. The college was most definitely swimming against the pro-Irish language tide. It did not seem to bother either the masters or the pupils and it was well into the twentieth century, and only then for a mere ten years or so, that Irish games were introduced.

Thomas enjoyed school life and excelled in his studies. By 1894 he indicated that he felt he had a vocation for the priesthood and, like other boys professing Holy Orders, he was transferred to a special house, called the Lake House, within the school grounds. His father died in that same year and soon he started to doubt his calling. His mother, of course, had been most supportive of her son's call to the church and was disappointed when he decided against the life of a priest. He did, however, become a teaching assistant and was given responsibilities with many of the younger boys. From all accounts he proved an excellent educator, even in those early years. He left Rockwell in 1901, aged 23, conscious of the fact that he had no priestly vocation and looked forward to whatever direction life would take him.

A first publication and the Gaelic League

Now in his early twenties, Thomas began to seriously consider publishing a book of his poetry. He had been writing, on and off, during his time at Rockwell and was driven to publish. In the meantime he had been appointed, in 1901, as senior master of English, History and French at St. Kieran's College in Kilkenny. The next year his first book appeared under the title *Through the Ivory*

Gate. But the book was a disappointment not only in sales but, more importantly, in his own eyes and estimation. He soon disowned the publication keeping only a couple of the poems which he had included in it. Thomas, although a popular teacher, was a morbid sort of young man. He felt that he had let his mother down by not taking Holy Orders and he knew that his loss of faith rankled with her. Although he remained a nominal Roman Catholic throughout his life, he certainly did not practise his faith.

He now started to concentrate on his teaching at St. Kieran's. The early 1900s were difficult years for the teaching profession. The campaign, spurred on by Douglas Hyde, to have Irish included in school curricula rumbled on although Thomas did not want to involve himself too much in what was going on. But, by the end of 1903, he had resigned from his post in Kilkenny. By this stage in his life he had joined the Gaelic League, another brainchild of Douglas Hyde, and had become an ardent member of the Kilkenny branch. Soon he became a committee member and began to work hard furthering the goals of the League. He attended, like so many other disciples of the Irish language, Irish classes which took place on Inishmaan, one of the Aran islands off the Galway coast. He immersed himself there and encouraged his friends and fellow Kilkenny colleagues to follow his example. In 1903 Thomas confidently put his name forward for election to the League's governing body but his nomination was unsuccessful. Feeling slighted, although he had no real reason for reacting that way, he lost interest in the League and considered another publication.

Thomas remembered how dissatisfied he had been with his first poetry book. It had not gone well and he had contacted W. B. Yeats, the distinguished Irish poet, for his advice. Yeats had been pleased that MacDonagh had asked him for help and guidance but Yeats told Thomas bluntly that his poetry was too conventional and lacked depth. He encouraged Thomas to read more and particularly some of the great English poets. Yeats thought it unwise to publish that first book, but Thomas had done so and even dedicated the work to Yeats. Now that some time had passed since that early, second-rate book had been published, Thomas was determined to make a success of his next work.

April and May with other verse came out at Easter 1903 but it was neither critically nor financially successful nor did it receive any reviews worth talking about. Thomas MacDonagh had still much to learn concerning the art of writing poetry. He was finding life in Kilkenny too stifling and made up his mind to seek a position elsewhere. He soon secured a post at St Colman's College in Fermoy in north county Cork. Once again he was invigorated by the fact that this school was totally immersed in the Irish language. Thomas responded by proving to be a popular master. He involved himself in the Gaelic League activities in Fermoy and soon became their secretary, treasurer and lecturer. But, once again, he quickly lost interest in the branch work and left before the end of 1904.

For the next three years, 1904 until 1907, he worked on his third book. He was, of course, conscious that his previous publications had not been successful, yet he was determined to move forward. This book was called *The Golden Joy* which finally appeared in 1907 after all sorts of difficulties in finding a publisher. Once more, however, he failed in his goal and still lacked any decent style in writing popular poetry. But he continued to persevere and wrote a libretto for a sacred piece written by an Italian, Bendetto Palmieri, entitled *The Exodus – Sacred Cantata*. It was performed at the Royal University on 19 May 1904 but the reviews, especially one submitted by Arthur Griffith, poured scorn on the work, declaring that it should never have won a prize since it had nothing to do with Ireland. The only tenuous connection was that an Irishman, Thomas MacDonagh, had written the words. Approaching his 30th birthday, Thomas had still not won the hearts and minds of the critics and the reading public. His poetry was still, at best, mediocre and, at worst, downright lacklustre.

Thomas MacDonagh was, if nothing else, tenacious and dogged. If poetry wouldn't work, then he would attempt a play. The title for his first piece in this genre was *When the dawn is come*. He had started writing this in 1904 but it was 1908 before it was complete enough to be accepted for production. He submitted the play to the burgeoning Abbey Theatre where it was accepted with changes. It was performed on stage for three nights in October 1908 but, predictably, the critics were not enthusiastic. There was, however, at least one favourable review and that was written for St Enda's school magazine. By 1908 he had resigned from St Colman's in Fermoy and had been taken on as a deputy headmaster at Patrick Pearse's Irish language school, St Enda's, which was situated at Cullenswood House in Ranelagh near to Dublin city centre. His move to join Pearse and the minor success of his first play encouraged Thomas.

Teaching at St Enda's suited Thomas very well. He quickly gained the reputation of being an excellent teacher and he greatly enjoyed the engagement with his pupils and their parents, many of whom were well known figures in Dublin. It now seemed to be de rigueur to send your son to Pearse's innovative establishment where the serious minded headmaster, Mr Pearse, was complemented by the easy going and humorous Mr MacDonagh. Thomas began to meet other influential people like Douglas Hyde, Maud Gonne, Padraic Colum and Edward Martyn and it was at this stage in his life that he met the Plunkett family and became friendly with Joseph. It was also through this contact that he met his future wife, Muriel Gifford.

1908 had been a busy year with his move from Fermoy to Dublin and his budding friendships with the Plunketts and Giffords. It was also the year of another family sorrow. Thomas's mother, Mary, died on 26 November, after a long illness. After her death Thomas rarely returned to the place of his childhood, the village of Cloughjordan. From then on his closest family contact would be with one of his sisters, Mary Josephine, who had become a nun, Sister Francesca.

New friendships and literary success

By 1909 Thomas had become disillusioned with the antics of the Gaelic League. He had worked hard for them in Kilkenny and Fermoy but, by the time he had reached Dublin, he considered his position within the movement and decided to distance himself from their squabbles and disagreements. Once more he concentrated on more writing. His association with Willie Yeats had blossomed and he felt more confident. He set about writing several articles for various publications and this time, at long last, they were judged as mature and a great improvement on his previous attempts. Yeats had no doubt helped him and he had obviously listened to his advice.

His circle of friends increased and Padraic Colum, a writer of some importance, met with Thomas often. Another acquaintance was Mary Maguire with whom Thomas fell in love. He even proposed to her more than once but was rejected each time. Thomas continued to grow in confidence particularly in the matter of his personal life. He was devastated when Mary decided to marry Colum, although, as it happened, Thomas was to marry before them. In 1910, he resigned from St Enda's mainly because Pearse was contemplating moving the school from Ranelagh out to the southern suburbs of the city at Rathfarnham. He did not fancy the idea of teaching out in the wilds of the countryside. And the fact that Mary had turned down his marriage proposals probably had something to do with his decision.

He left St Enda's without having secured another job which was considered rash and out of character and moved to live in Paris for some months in the summer of that year. He greatly enjoyed living in the French capital with its cafes and galleries and its pretty women. He was, from his Rockwell days of course, fluent in French and fitted in very comfortably. It was an experience he would not forget.

He returned to Dublin in September 1910 and took up residence at Grange House Lodge which, believe it or not, was next door to the Hermitage where Pearse had moved his school.

On account, therefore, of his close proximity to the school, Thomas started to undertake some further teaching duties there. He was glad of the chance to get back and was welcomed back by students and teachers alike. Pearse himself would also have been pleased to see his friend return. He had been missed.

His fourth book, *Songs of Myself*, was published in the autumn of 1910 with limited success. His style of writing was slowly improving thanks to help and advice from Yeats and Colum. From this time on he became very close to Joseph Plunkett whose health was always giving rise to concern. The Plunkett family was a wealthy one and so Joseph had no problems visiting Europe and north Africa in the hope that his delicate condition would improve. When Joseph was abroad Thomas regularly kept in touch with him by letter and their friendship grew from strength to strength.

Marriage and beyond

Thomas fell in love with Muriel Gifford and married her on 3 January 1911. Theirs had been a whirlwind romance and, though there were problems within the families because Muriel was a protestant (and remained so throughout most of her life) and Thomas was, at least nominally, a Roman Catholic, the young pair seemed well matched. Both families eventually accepted the marriage and became friends as the years went by. By the time of his marriage, Thomas had been furthering his education. He had successfully completed a BA at University College in 1909 and then embarked on his MA. He undertook a difficult thesis on the English poet, Thomas Campion, and, for his excellent dissertation, was awarded a First Class Honours degree. Many scholars at the university and beyond poured praise on Thomas for his work and the thesis was considered so good that it was published in February 1913. He felt elated and full of confidence and applied for the vacant chair of History and English at University College, Galway. However his euphoria was to be short-lived when his application was turned down.

Thomas MacDonagh had not given up hope of becoming one of Ireland's premier playwrights. In November 1911 he had completed his second play which he entitled *Metempsychosis* and it was performed by some breakaway Abbey actors in the Hardwicke Hall Theatre for three nights in April 1912. It received a further airing in the same theatre a year later in May 1913. The play, whose main character appeared to be a close portrayal of Willie Yeats (from whom Thomas was now partly estranged), was not a success and was not well received by the audiences.

Thomas now became involved in the publication of a monthly magazine entitled *The Irish Review*. Padraic Colum was a leading light in this journal and invited Thomas to help and to write articles for the paper. He happily obliged and for three years from 1911 until 1914 it was a great success. During this period Thomas published his fifth book called *Lyrical Poems* which was a compilation of many of his earlier poems together with around twenty new ones. It was an impressive volume, partly subsidised by *The Irish Review*. Thomas MacDonagh's star at last appeared to be in the ascendant although, in truth, his poetry was still described as mediocre and his composition as yet disappointing. The book was considered as a 'noble failure'.

The Plunketts had bought the paper in 1913 when it had started to struggle for funds and copy. When the Volunteer movement took off at the end of 1913, with membership quickly reaching upwards of 200,000, the journal sold well and it became, to all intents and purposes, the propaganda sheet for the Volunteers. But the original bias of the paper became eroded and it ceased publication during 1914. Colum and MacDonagh had nothing to be ashamed of since lots of newspapers and journals like theirs were rising and falling as readership waxed and waned especially throughout these turbulent years in Ireland before partition.

Thomas and Muriel were overjoyed when their son, Donagh, was born on 22 November 1912. However Muriel became ill after a difficult delivery and suffered from recurrent illnesses for many months to come. Thomas helped out at home as much as he could and was pleased to be near at hand as he had by then been employed as an academic at University College, Dublin. Around this time Thomas wrote and had published his last book. *Literature in Ireland* had taken him a long time to complete and it was not, in fact, brought out until after his death. This title, namely on account of the poignancy associated with his martyr's death, has remained, even until today, MacDonagh's best-known work. The content of the book was still short on style and organisation but, nonetheless, had a certain amount of merit.

Joining the Volunteers before a martyr's death

When Eoin MacNeill delivered his first speech to the newly formed Irish Volunteers at the Rotunda on 25 November 1913, Thomas MacDonagh was not in the vast audience. He probably had intended to be there but circumstances prevented him from experiencing the thrill and excitement of that inaugural gathering. But it was not long before he was deeply involved taking up the reins as commandant of 'C' Company of the 2nd Dublin Battalion within a few short weeks. Then, and in addition, he was appointed Director General of Training with responsibility for recruitment to the organisation. He proved most effective in this important role and attracted hundreds of new recruits in double quick time. It should be remembered that, from the very outset, Thomas was not a physical force man which seemed incongruous and inconsistent with the job he held.

It is timely to note that Thomas MacDonagh, regardless of the vital recruiting role he held in the Volunteer organisation, was not a member of the secret military council which consisted of the other leading lights, Pearse, MacDermott, Clarke, Plunkett and Ceannt. Students of Ireland's history of this era will know that there were seven signatories to the Proclamation on Easter Monday 1916, but neither MacDonagh nor Connolly were original, or even early, members of that exclusive group. In fact it was not until a couple of weeks before the Rising that MacDonagh was admitted to the inner sanctum of the military council. Many debates and discussions took place, and many have since taken place, about the timing of MacDonagh's inclusion in that fateful group. There are those who cannot, and will not, believe he did not know of the plans for the Rising until April 1916 yet just as many who declare the opposite to be the truth. On reflection it would sound correct that he was ignorant of the arrangements until the last minute. The reasons remain the subject of debate and argument but, in all his writings, he denies any prior knowledge. It matters little, however, for when the Rising did erupt the name of Thomas MacDonagh appeared clearly amongst the other signatures. Whether he was an early or a late signatory hardly matters; he met the same fate as the others at the conclusion of that momentous Easter week.

Although his involvement in the Volunteers did take centre stage after 1914, Thomas was still writing and his play *Pagans* was performed at the Hardwicke Hall for a week in April 1915. Along with Joseph Plunkett and Edward Martyn, he had formed the Irish Theatre Company in direct opposition to the Abbey Theatre. However, like so much that he had become involved in throughout his life, the venture was not successful. They did try to offer a different kind of production at the Hardwicke but the public still seemed unimpressed. MacDonagh had plenty of other matters to fill his time and, whilst he wanted to improve and make alterations to *Pagans*, these revisions were never completed.

The Easter Rising 1916

By the outbreak of the Rising on Easter Monday 1916, Thomas MacDonagh was fully involved in what was to happen. Like Pearse and the other signatories to the Proclamation, he was outraged at MacNeill's countermanding of the orders for manoeuvres on Easter Day. As instructed he led his company of the 2nd Battalion of the Volunteers to Jacob's Biscuit Factory from their assembly point close to St Stephen's Green. He had around 160 men and women with him as he entered the factory, expelling the workers as they took up their positions on the roof of the high building. The choice of Jacob's was then, and has remained so since, a mystery. It was not in any way a strategic location and saw little or no action throughout that auspicious week. The occupants were inactive within the vast and eerie building; the nervous commandant, MacDonagh and his more militarily experienced second in command, John MacBride, did what they could to keep up the morale of their company; the limited diet of biscuits and confectionary left them all hungry and restless.

When ordered to surrender on the Sunday, MacDonagh refused to accept without first consulting the British General Lowe who promptly assured him that Patrick Pearse had agreed to an unconditional surrender. The battalion laid down their arms and were marched off to the Rotunda to await their fate. Thomas MacDonagh had not long to contemplate his future. He was court-martialled on 2 May and, along with Pearse and Clarke, was shot by firing squad in the grounds of Kilmainham Jail the next day, 3 May 1916. He was not permitted to see his wife, Muriel, and his two children, Donagh and Barbara (little Barbara had been born on 24 March 1915), prior to his execution but was granted a visit from his sister, Mary, the nun Sister Francesca, in the few hours before he was shot. In the end he did receive the comfort of the Roman Catholic Church.

After the execution, Muriel and the children almost became destitute for Thomas had left only a very meagre sum in his will. The little family went to Thurles to live with Joseph MacDonagh, her brother-in-law, until eventually, with the help of donations for those bereaved by the aftermath of the Rising, she was able to return to Dublin. Sadly Muriel did not survive her husband by long. On 9 July 1917, just over a year since Thomas's death, she drowned in the sea near Skerries attempting to swim out to an offshore island. Muriel had been converted to Roman Catholicism and received into the church at Easter that year. The children consequently had an unhappy childhood and greatly suffered from the loss of their parents in such a short time. They were drawn to and fro between both families which made for a most traumatic upbringing.

Thomas's final works were posthumously published in *The Poetical Works of Thomas MacDonagh* and appeared during the summer of 1916. This book became popular mainly as a martyr's memorial. He will be best remembered, not as a poet and playwright, as he would have wanted, but as one of the signatories of the Proclamation of the Easter Rising. His name, whilst not entirely forgotten, still ranks significantly lower than the names of Patrick Pearse, Tom Clarke and James Connolly. His life, however, was an interesting one. He was a determined young man who aspired to the heights of one of Ireland's premier literary geniuses. Whether he succeeded is up to the reader to decide.

Suggested reading
1. Martin, F. X. (ed), *Leaders and Men of the Easter Rising: Dublin 1916*, London, 1967.
2. Norstedt, Johann, *Thomas MacDonagh – a Critical Biography*, Charlottesville, 1980.
3. Shannon, M., *Sixteen Roads to Golgotha – the Life Stories of the Sixteen Executed Leaders of the Easter Rising*, Dublin, c. 1965.

Michael Collins

Passionate and patriotic – the man of
the moment

The name of Michael Collins is known to anyone who has even the slightest interest in Ireland and especially of those critical years from 1916-1921; his name is always associated with the struggle of the Anglo-Irish war and the early days of the partition of Ireland. He died young and has consequently become, to many, a true folk hero. To others he may have been an opportunist and there were those, too, who even reviled his very name. Yet, regardless of whether or not you agree with him, his is certainly a story of action, courage and audacity.

He was born on 16 October 1890 at his home place called Woodfield, near Sam's Cross not far from the town of Clonakilty in west county Cork. He was the youngest of eight children, three sons and five daughters, of Michael and Marianne. Michael Collins senior did not marry until he was 60 years old which was not such a surprising occurrence in rural Ireland in those days. Often the eldest son had to wait until his father died before inheriting the family farm and such was the case at Woodfield. Marianne, nee O'Brien, his new wife, was just 23 when they married. In terms of Roman Catholic families Michael Collins was well to do with 90 acres of good land. He was the seventh son of a seventh son and was well-educated and good at mathematics. But his prime concern was for the farm and the profit he could make now that he had a large family to support.

Young Michael was born when his father was already 75 years old yet he learnt a great deal from him. The old man was fit enough and was able to handle his farm duties well. Michael senior died in 1897 when his youngest boy was just six years old. Mrs Collins, who was an ambitious and hard working woman, immediately set about building a new stone farmhouse which was completed in good time. She had many good neighbours, many of them protestants, who all helped at the time of her husband's death. She counted herself fortunate to be rearing her thriving family with so many good friends surrounding her.

Michael's schooling and early influences

Michael started school at Lisavaird before he was even four years old. He had a very influential teacher, Denis Lyons, who was not only a brilliant schoolmaster but also a man who was keen to impart to his pupils, including young Michael, true Irish patriotism. He was a member of the Irish Republican Brotherhood (IRB) and was a typical Fenian. When Michael would go home from school he would often call at the forge of James Santry who would further inculcate nationalist principles into the young lad.

Michael left his little school and was enrolled at Clonakilty National School. As the town was quite a distance from his home, young Michael stayed with his sister, Margaret, who lived in Clonakilty with her husband, Patrick O'Driscoll, who was the publisher of *The West Cork People*. Whilst attending school, where he was an avid reader studying, amongst others, Arthur Griffith's writings, he also helped O'Driscoll by reporting events for his newspaper. But, like so many bright scholars at schools throughout west Cork, Michael was being prepared to sit the British Civil Service examination for entrance as a clerk in the Post Office. At age 15 he duly passed the examination and travelled to London in July 1906 to start his job in West Kensington Post Office. Once more he was able to live with another family member, his older sister, Hannie, who was also working in London.

However back at home, great sadness touched the Collins family when Mrs Marianne Collins died from cancer at the early age of 54. Michael's eldest brother, John, took over the family farm and lived there until the Essex Regiment torched the homestead in 1921 during the War of Independence.

In London, although influenced by the British way of life to some extent, Michael kept up his interest in Irish affairs. He quickly became involved in various Irish activities soon joining the Gaelic Athletic Association (GAA) to play football and hurling. His good friend and cousin, Sean Hurley, joined at the same time. Michael's propensity for hard work and involvement in the administration of organisations led him quickly to become treasurer of his club, the Geraldines. He became acquainted with the famous Sam Maguire (who, incidentally, was a protestant) who swore the young Collins into the IRB.

Michael worked at the Post Office for four years until 1910 before resigning to join a firm of stockbrokers, Horne and Company of Moorgate and, a further four more years later in 1914, he went to the Board of Trade as a clerk. He was clearly a determined and ambitious young man. He may have been like the west Cork lads who joined the Post Office (and usually stayed all their working lives there) but when he saw an opportunity for advancement, he readily accepted it.

While he was in London his sister tried to keep a tight rein on her younger brother. She discouraged him from involving himself in political activities and did her best to divert his attentions by introducing him to her friends. The tactic only had limited success. Michael became a ladies' man and had a number of girlfriends, and at the same time he had the incredible good luck in meeting many society women including Lady Hazel Lavery and even Lady Edith Londonderry. These contacts were to be of real significance later in his life.

By the time the Great War broke out in 1914 Michael had been working in London for eight years. He had, from time to time, managed to make a few visits home in order to keep up his contacts there. But he realised that he could be conscripted and there was also talk that he might travel to work in the United States with his brother, Patrick. But this opportunity did not work out and he changed his job yet again, in 1915, when he went to work for an American firm which had an office in London. But the situation was becoming critical with regard to a possible call up. He then made a momentous decision by telling his employers that he was going to join the fight. They congratulated and supported him, little realising that his fight would not be for the British forces but for the impending struggle in his own homeland. Consequently he headed off for Ireland in January 1916, fully nine and a half years after setting foot in London back in 1906. The die was cast. His sister was most unhappy and said that no good would come of his returning to Dublin. Perhaps she was right; only time would tell.

With his contacts in London and his keen political mind, Michael knew that the IRB was planning a rebellion and he wanted to be part of it. Home Rule was still a distinct possibility as the third parliamentary bill would soon be on the Statute Book. The time was ripe to make a move so he immediately came to the notice, not yet of the British intelligence forces, but of those in charge of the IRB. He got a job in Dublin but spent his spare time helping Count Plunkett with financial matters. He joined various organisations and got to know men like Richard Mulcahy, Cathal Brugha and Rory O'Connor as well as many others. Some would remain friends; others would become sworn enemies. He was a typical young enthusiast in those early days revering, amongst others, Tom Clarke and even Roger Casement. Activists in the Irish capital quickly realised that young Michael Collins was more than just an ordinary adherent to the cause. He was clearly of leadership material. They knew at once that he would be a force with which to be reckoned.

The Easter Rising

Michael Collins' Easter Rising was spent in the General Post Office, the headquarters of the insurgents. He had been allocated a number of jobs and he stuck religiously to his tasks and carried out his orders to the letter. Firstly he had to assist the sickly Joseph Plunkett (one of the signatories who suffered from TB and who had just returned from treatment in Switzerland) to the Metropole Hotel so that he would be near the GPO. Then Collins joined Pearse and Connolly at Liberty Hall before setting off for Sackville (later to be O'Connell) Street and the Post Office on that fateful Easter Monday, 24 April 1916. There his duties were in the operations room where he remained until the order was given to evacuate the burning building on the following Friday. He heard the devastating news that his dear friend, Sean Hurley, had been killed in the fighting and he was despondent and sad. He was marched off after the surrender to Richmond Barracks. But he was not fingered by the 'G' men, the British intelligence force, as a leader. They had missed their chance. The future mighty thorn in the British flesh, young Michael Collins, was still an unknown amongst the masses of captured prisoners. So he escaped court martial and execution.

Collins, with many others, was sent to Stafford jail in England and there he first encountered the so-called 'university of revolution'. Soon he was moved to Frongoch camp in north Wales and it was here that the name of Michael Collins became well known and notorious. He immediately set about encouraging and browbeating his fellow prisoners into making good use of their time in captivity and learn. During these months, under Collins's leadership, many Irishmen became converts to the cause of Irish separation from Britain. They could thank the likeable and exuberant Michael Collins for their radical change of heart. By Christmas 1916 an amnesty had been announced and the men from Frongoch, and most of the other prisoners kept in various British jails, were released. Michael Collins was free again but his mind was made up. There would be no more bungled rebellions like the one the previous Easter. A more careful and determined effort now needed to be made, and Michael Collins was resolved to take a lead part in it.

His return to Ireland

Michael's arrival back home to Woodfield turned out to be a sad affair as his grandmother had just died in the days coming up to Christmas. He was glad to leave his home and return to the action in Dublin. By this time Collins knew that the days of the old Irish Parliamentary Party were numbered. He was a physical force man and no longer a constitutionalist, if he ever had actually been one. He turned to the new politics and set about, with his noted vigour, into the campaign to get Count Plunkett elected in the north Roscommon seat. Plunkett's bid was successful although he had no intention of taking his seat at Westminster. This decision was mirrored by candidates in other forthcoming by-elections. Although Collins was prominent in the Plunkett campaign he was conspicuous by his absence from the de Valera fight in east Clare in the summer of 1917.

His non-attendance would have been noted but he had other work to do and in his endeavours he was most conscientious. He actively organised volunteers; he established links with Irish Americans; he encouraged membership of the IRB; and he arranged a gun smuggling network between Ireland and sympathisers in Great Britain. Michael Collins was never idle and, for a long time, he had one Joe O'Reilly as his right hand man. The depth and strength of the young Michael Collins was duly noted both by his revolutionary colleagues and by the men at Dublin Castle. From now on he would have to watch his step and keep ahead of the chasing pack.

The secret Collins

Michael Collins now set out on a very dangerous mission. He made plans to infiltrate the spy network at Dublin Castle. He knew that if he had inside information he could make good use of it. And so he surrounded himself with a small number of accomplices, men whom he could trust with his life. Ned Broy, David Neligan and Joe Kavanagh were closest to him and nothing was put in motion without these men's advices. They had contacts which were imparted to Collins regularly. He also was aware of the need to find an insider if at all possible. His luck was in for he had none other than a second cousin of his, Nancy O'Brien, actually working in the castle administration and she was prepared to assist Collins regardless of the danger to herself. She copied a great deal of vital information which she passed to Collins.

The threat of conscription still loomed large over all of Ireland throughout 1918. The numbers of soldiers being killed and put out of action in the killing fields of France was rising at an alarming rate. Conscription seemed the only alternative. But the

British had not reckoned with the outcry against such a move. It came, not only from the republican element in Irish society, but also from both churches and from many in the north. It was an unpopular suggestion which eventually came to naught. Many young Irishmen had already joined up since the war began, both from the unionist north and the nationalist south, and thousands had been killed or injured. The British were taken aback by the vociferousness of the anti-conscription campaign and so dropped the idea. Thankfully the war finished before 1918 was out.

Collins was briefly arrested in April 1918 but he used his consummate skills of bluff to attain his almost immediate release. He appreciated that he was of more help outside prison than inside so he made it his aim never to be taken again. By this time his own network of agents had broken the spy system in the castle and his star was in the ascendancy amongst his colleagues. He was appointed Director of Operations and Adjutant General before the year was out. By the middle of the year the British were cracking down on all sorts of Irish activities even forbidding language classes, playing Irish sports and Irish dancing. In the month of May a number of Collins' colleagues, Griffith, Figgis and Plunkett, were arrested although Collins evaded capture by being 'on the run' on his bicycle. Whilst most other of the senior men were incarcerated, Collins was able to carry on with the help of his own squad.

The war ended in November 1918 and a General Election was imminent. This was, of course, a great opportunity for the Irish Party to be thoroughly defeated and this became reality when 73 of the so-called Sinn Feiners were chosen by the electorate. The Irish Party, as predicted, was decimated with just seven MPs elected, down dramatically from the previous number of almost 80 representatives. By this time John Redmond their leader had died leaving the party in turmoil.

Michael Collins now advanced from strength to strength and was instrumental in instigating many bold initiatives. With the assistance of those closest to him he smuggled arms, improved his intelligence network, established a hit squad and bomb making factories, and even founded two underground newspapers. And all the time he was 'on the run' with those hunting him not even certain of what he looked like. He did lead a charmed life but fortune seemingly did favour the brave. Even with all this pressure his innate concern for ordinary people showed itself. He visited families who needed assistance and advice and, during the eighteen months when de Valera was absent in America from the summer of 1919 until the end of 1920, Michael Collins continued to visit Sinead de Valera and her family. Collins evidently seemed never to sleep yet he pursued his goals with a strength of mind unrivalled amongst his peers. His favourite way to let off steam was what he called 'a bit of ear' when he wrestled with his often reluctant friends. Those who knew Michael Collins well realised what a special person he was. To many he was a god and he was hero worshipped by most of the younger men who surrounded him.

The legend of Michael Collins was further enhanced when he involved himself in the 'springing' of Eamon de Valera from Lincoln Jail and Robert Barton from Dublin's Mountjoy prison during 1919. On 21 January 1919 those who were elected in the landslide poll of December 1918 met together in Dublin to form Dail Eireann. This was, of course, an illegal parliament but nonetheless those members who were not in jail or 'on the run', just 28 in total, set up their embryonic seat of government. None of the Unionist members or the few remaining of the Irish Party deigned to make an appearance although they were invited. Collins was a member but, as was absolutely necessary, kept a low profile. However he was immediately given the important task of raising funds to keep their organisation afloat. He was very successful in his endeavours whilst still managing to evade capture by the British. He was nearly caught one day at the Dail and, had it not been for the vigilance of his friend Ned Broy, he surely would have been in custody. And it was Broy who was able to get Collins smuggled into the Brunswick Street police headquarters where all the most secret government files were held. Over a number of nights ensconced inside he made very good use of all the extremely sensitive material he found there. From the documentation gathered he was from then on able to put pressure on the 'G' men and frequently used threats and blackmail to further his ends. It is reputed that he even read his own file whilst sifting through the archives.

During all these difficult and critical days of late 1919 and throughout 1920, Eamon de Valera, styling himself as the President of Ireland, was in America. There he tried to raise funds for the Irish cause but only with a limited degree of success. He fought and struggled with the Irish American lobby there and, although he did make some friends and make some progress, his long stay there was considered rather unsatisfactory. Accompanying de Valera on his trip was Harry Boland, a bosom friend of Collins. They had known each other for some time and had formed a close relationship. It even appeared that both men had fallen in love with the same young woman, Kitty Kiernan, from Granard in county Longford; it was even reputed that they were both actually engaged to Kitty at the same time. However, as the time went on, Boland and Collins drifted apart and ended up taking diametrically opposed stances, ending tragically for both men.

The hero, Michael Collins

In the meantime, back in Ireland where the action was, Michael Collins took on the mantle of popular hero. It was during these troubled days of 1920 that he made his name, a name that is still remembered to this day. He had been elected as President of the IRB and this position within the organisation was to stand him in good stead during the Treaty talks which took place in the autumn of 1921. He was still barely 30 years old.

It was now that the ruthless side of Collins became all too apparent. He was determined that the Dail's writ should take precedence over the King's in Ireland. He realised that this could mean taking out of circulation many of the spies who continued to baulk his efforts. He therefore decided that his squad of men, his so-called elite twelve 'apostles', should be given the task, only when absolutely necessary, to eliminate these 'G' men. But his men were not criminal killers. Collins therefore insisted that they be temperate and should not have revenge in their hearts. And so it was that during the fateful year of 1920 the squad would exact retribution on their enemies in the castle.

The War of Independence, or the Anglo-Irish War, or the Black and Tan War, had erupted with a vengeance. The fight for independence had taken a physical force turn. For the first time guerrilla warfare would be used in Ireland. In an endeavour to quell this insurrection, the British resorted to the use of men who had recently returned from fighting in the Great War. They were recruited in a hurry, were kitted out in a motley selection of uniform and became known as the Black and Tans, the name of a famous pack of foxhounds in the west of Ireland. They were well paid, but had a detestable job in a country with which they were not familiar. Consequently the fight turned into an ugly one further exacerbated by the arrival soon afterwards of the Auxiliaries, or the 'Auxies', who had been recruited from the ranks of unemployed officers. Their attitude to the indigenous Irish was even more brutal and cruel. The scene was set for a vicious and bloody struggle.

Collins appreciated the magnitude of the forthcoming struggle. He knew he could depend on the loyalty of his squad in Dublin but he also knew how important it was to have men throughout the country willing to take on the British forces. These flying columns of young men roamed the countryside attacking the Black and Tans as they roared through sleepy Irish towns and villages in their armoured cars creating havoc wherever they went. It may have seemed an unequal struggle but this was not the case. The volunteers captured and burnt nearly all the police stations in the land; they successfully disrupted the British systems of justice and administration; they helped local politicians win municipal elections throughout the southern and western counties. However, in turn, the Black and Tans inflicted reprisals upon the population by burning towns and torching local businesses. They shot dead the Lord Mayors of Cork and Limerick on their doorsteps. The country was in turmoil. Yet in the midst of it all, Michael Collins, still of course remaining elusive and moving from one secret location to another, a favourite being Devlin's public house in Parnell Square, carried the fight to the ever more frustrated British garrison. He remained a complex character and, although he was mostly friendly with those he met, yet he did possess a foul temper and would not stand unpunctuality.

Collins never relished the idea of killing spies but he did realise that this extreme action might be necessary in some circumstances. He was, of course, a firm advocate of guerrilla warfare unlike his Dail colleague, the irascible Cathal Brugha. They argued incessantly about the best way to approach the struggle against the British, with Collins promoting the guerrilla campaign and with Brugha, hard as it is to believe, pushing for full frontal attacks against the enemy. This was totally unrealistic yet Brugha still persisted. Whilst they fought it out in various secret locations, the Black and Tans were continuing to cause mayhem with picturesque towns like Balbriggan, Thurles and Lahinch being sacked and destroyed. 1920 proved to be very troubled year with more than 200 innocent civilians being murdered, mostly by Crown forces. Collins did orchestrate actions on the British mainland with, for example, a number of warehouses being destroyed on one night. Towards the end of that awful year several notorious events took place.

Shame, destruction and bloody murder
On 25 October 1920 Terence McSwiney, the Lord Mayor of Cork, died following a 74 day hunger strike in an English jail and a week later, on All Saints Day, 1 November, the 18 year old Kevin Barry was executed. These horrific events caused outrage, not only in Ireland but much further afield. Barry instantly became yet another of Ireland's martyrs, even being put to death by the insensitive

British on one of the church's most revered and holy days. All even-minded people throughout the British Isles sympathised with the prolonged agony of McSwiney in Brixton Prison in London as his life slowly ebbed away during probably the longest fast to death ever endured by any prisoner.

It was time for Collins to act. He reviled the excesses of the British and was determined to deal a deadly blow which would cripple the Dublin Castle administration before they could close in on him. On so-called Bloody Sunday, 21 November, he sent out his squad into Dublin where they shot fourteen agents in their beds in various parts of the city. Many of those killed died in front of their wives or mistresses. It was a coordinated strike which struck terror into the heart of the castle's spy network. In that one night the espionage arm of the British was virtually severed although Collins' day was tinged with sadness as, later that same night, three of his friends, including a young Gaelic scholar who was visiting the city, were captured by the Auxiliaries and brutally done to death. Collins was so upset that he took the huge risk of attending the funeral masses for his deceased friends. He realised how dangerous this was as all entrances to the churches were being watched but he knew what he had to do.

But that Sunday in November was also to go down in Irish history for yet another heinous outrage. During the afternoon at Croke Park, two counties, Tipperary and Dublin, were playing football. Suddenly a number of armoured cars, driven by Black and Tans and Auxiliaries, crashed through the gates, drove onto the pitch and began firing into the crowd. In the mayhem and confusion that followed, fourteen innocent fans and one Tipperary player, Michael Hogan, were killed and over 60 wounded. It was a day of infamy and shame for Ireland, one which would never be forgotten. In 1924 the new stand at Croke Park was named 'The Hogan Stand' in memory of the young player who had died on the pitch that day.

Michael Collins knew that he had done exactly what he had set out to do. The hated Cairo gang of British spies had been eliminated. He sorrowed, as did W. T. Cosgrave and the rest of the Dail cabinet, at the unnecessary deaths of so many innocent people but he continued on ruthlessly with his plans. The following Sunday, 28 November, a pre-emptive strike taken by Tom Barry's flying column at Kilmichael in county Cork succeeded in killing 17 soldiers in an ambush. Collins' brother, Johnny, had taken part in the planning of this attack. Before the end of the year, the spectacular burning of large parts of the city of Cork, proved, if it was ever in doubt, that British reprisals still could have a significant effect on the life of a country struggling to survive. However 1921 would not bring any respite, rather the contrary. Death and destruction would continue to stalk the land.

1921 – an even more brutal year

Eamon de Valera eventually returned to Ireland at Christmas 1920, having spent eighteen months in America. He was hardly home when he suggested to Michael Collins that he should go there himself to continue the work that de Valera had started. Collins would have nothing to do with it. He considered the hard and dangerous work he had carried out during possibly Ireland's most oppressive year and a half and he told de Valera, in no uncertain terms, that he had no intention of leaving Ireland. It was clear that de Valera, having missed out on the action, wanted to banish Collins and carry on where Collins had left off. But Collins was resolute and remained to make further progress. He let de Valera see who was boss. This attitude did not go down well with de Valera or with Collins' archenemy, Cathal Brugha. This man was supposed to be Minister of Defence, but did little work and did not know his men. Collins warned de Valera that he would not stand for Brugha's negative attitude and would leave Dublin and take to the hills with his Cork men. Even de Valera realised how disastrous this would be and encouraged Collins not to quit his valuable work in Dublin. De Valera had much to be grateful for in regard to Michael Collins for he appreciated that, during his sojourn in America, Collins had religiously visited his family spending lots of time there playing with his children. Yet, despite acknowledging and respecting de Valera's position within the organisation, the two men could not get on and many of his leader's appointments, like that of President designate to Austin Stack, another dinosaur in Collins's estimation, and the defection of his good friend, Harry Boland to the de Valera side, irked him constantly.

For Collins, and of course Ireland, life continued to be most disruptive. His home place at Woodfield was razed to the ground by Crown forces in April, which meant that his brother, Johnny, and his large family were now homeless. Countless awful and brutal killings were inflicted on the population by the Black and Tans. Some of their tactics were beyond the pale including the dastardly act of tying a number of prisoners together and blowing them up. Collins made plans to kidnap members of the British cabinet and to hold them hostage but this came to nothing. There were proposals for a truce both from the British and from Collins. Even Pope Benedict pleaded with both sides to call a halt to all the cruel and futile murders even going as far as threatening excommunication for those involved. But the year progressed with little real chance of peace for a war torn country

By May 1921 the situation was as bad as ever. De Valera wanted to be more confrontational with the British. Collins, whose guerrilla campaign had already caused untold trouble for the British, insisted that this was the way forward. His men had little ammunition and so ambushing the enemy would preclude the necessity of having to use up vast amounts of, what was by now, a near dearth of bullets and explosives. But de Valera's madcap view prevailed and an attack was mounted on the Dublin Custom House. It might have yielded a good deal of propaganda but it was a military disaster. They lost six men dead, twelve wounded and over seventy captured. This effectively put an end to any further action and Collins could only hold his head in shame for his organisation. They were saved by the impending General Election.

All the southern seats were held, unopposed, by the Nationalists and Sinn Fein, apart from the Trinity College Unionists, and, in the north, forty Ulster Unionists and twelve Sinn Feiners took the 52 seats in the new Northern Ireland parliament.

The truce and the Treaty talks

A truce was called on 11 July 1921. The catalyst for this breakthrough was King George V. In his speech at Belfast City Hall when he opened the first northern legislature, the king appealed to all the warring factions throughout the country to lay down their arms and consider peace, something the people earnestly desired. The royal plea succeeded and arms were laid down. At the same time de Valera agreed to visit the British Prime Minister, David Lloyd George, to talk about the future of Ireland and Great Britain. Although de Valera had a strong enough team accompanying him, including Griffith, Barton, Stack, Childers and Plunkett, he totally ignored them and spent his time with Lloyd George on his own. He insisted on an immediate republic which, predictably, the British opposed. The party returned to Dublin without an agreement of any kind. The whole affair had been a complete waste of time, something which, of course, did not surprise the one cabinet colleague who should have been there, Michael Collins.

By now the partition of Ireland was a reality with James Craig in charge in Belfast and a new administration there keen on making progress. Lloyd George was anxious that more talks take place as quickly as possible. With his legendary skill of getting his opponents to change their minds, he was able to inveigle de Valera into a further conference between the two sides with the lesser threat of an Ireland with just tenuous links to the British Commonwealth. The tactic worked and de Valera prepared for further talks to start in early October. But, as with everything associated with de Valera, there was a twist when it came to choosing his representatives. On this occasion the team was not to be led by their leader who opted to stay at home. De Valera chose Arthur Griffith and Michael

Collins as leaders to be accompanied by Robert Barton, Eamonn Duggan and George Gavan Duffy. Collins, although disappointed at not being chosen for the abortive July talks, was now reluctant to go but was prevailed upon and joined his colleagues. These five men had the responsibility laid on their shoulders to return with an acceptable agreement. De Valera was, and still is today, castigated for not attending these crucial talks. He was criticised roundly yet, in retrospect, it was just as well that he did not go for he only would have accepted a republic and a complete severance between Ireland and the United Kingdom. This was unrealistic and de Valera's decision was probably the worst one he ever made in his life. He thought he could influence his delegates from far off Dublin and be able to isolate Griffith and Collins. But he had not reckoned with the grit and fortitude of these determined men. Although Griffith was chosen as the actual leader of the Irish delegation, it was Collins who assumed the leadership mainly on account of Griffith's poor health, and his own single-mindedness. He took with him to London a number of bodyguards and had accommodation at 15 Cadogan Gardens separate from the rest of the Irish party. This was a deliberate ploy for he knew he needed to keep his colleagues in Dublin abreast of what was happening without the interference of the other delegates. And there was still a bounty on his head; his chances of being assassinated were still very high on the agenda. He had to be careful and he was determined to be so.

The Treaty talks started on 11 October 1921. The Irish delegation, with its secretaries who included Erskine Childers and John Chartres, two men with an Anglo-Irish background, entered the room at Downing Street to be confronted by a veritable 'who's who' of eminent British politicians. Led by the Welsh wizard David Lloyd George, the others included Lord Birkenhead, Winston Churchill and Austen Chamberlain. They constituted a formidable force but, it has to be said, they in no way tried to intimidate the much less experienced Irishmen who felt, naturally enough, ill at ease.

For the first two weeks both sides met in full plenary session discussing various thorny issues such as trade, the relationship with the Crown and Northern Ireland. Not a lot of progress was being made which concerned Lloyd George. Consequently he suggested that meetings should go into sub committees with only Griffith and Collins taking part alongside two or three of the British ministers. This actually suited the Irish pair because they felt they could get on more expeditiously with the business and, more importantly, they could keep Childers out of these discussions. Collins, in particular, was convinced that Childers was a spy for de Valera who would immediately report back to his leader in Dublin. Collins returned to Dublin most weekends to report to his IRB colleagues on the state of the talks, but not, of course, the substance. When he was there de Valera constantly tried to interfere so much so that Collins threatened to pull out of the talks.

Back in London the wily Lloyd George was doing his best to hem Griffith in with vague promises. Collins was now hearing that de Valera had come up with another of his weird ideas which he called 'external association'. This suggested only a loose attachment of Britain and Ireland with Ireland no longer being a member of the Commonwealth. Lloyd George would have nothing of this and, in truth, both Griffith and Collins also agreed that this idea was a non-runner. By the middle of November there was virtual deadlock at the talks. To get the Irish off the hook a proposal was mooted that a Boundary Commission would be set up to decide on the final border within the partitioned Ireland. It was thought that large tracts of the new Northern Ireland with nationalist majorities would simply revert to the Irish Free State thus meaning that Northern Ireland would be too small to exist. This offer allowed the talks to proceed.

By the end of November the pressure on Collins was horrendous. Griffith was unwell: de Valera in Dublin was doing all he could to muddy the waters; Lloyd George was beginning to turn the screw. The responsibility for concluding, or terminating, the discussions fell solely on Michael Collins. When the delegation returned to Dublin over the weekend at the start of December each member was extremely tired. A cabinet meeting was held without allowing them time to rest. The meeting was acrimonious; the discussions fraught and the atmosphere, even amongst the delegates themselves, bitter and spiteful. De Valera was still arguing over the oath which the British insisted on including in the agreement. The delegates even returned to London on separate boats such was the hostility amongst them.

When they arrived in London, David Lloyd George, realising that great tension was in the air, pressed for a speedy conclusion to the talks. The British demanded that there be no more delay and that they would only give a short period for the agreement to be signed. They even threatened the Irish with a resumption of hostilities. Collins and Griffith knew that decision time had come and that they must now sign. It took time, during the early hours of 6 December at their hotel, to persuade Gavan Duffy, Duggan and especially Barton to affix their signatures to the Treaty. Eventually they did and the British were cock-a-hoop. Their pressure had worked; the Irish delegates had signed; the Treaty was assured. They congratulated Collins particularly on his determination but he told them that he had virtually signed his own death warrant. Little did he know that his ominous prediction would prove correct.

The Treaty debates and the aftermath

No sooner had the delegates arrived back in Dublin than chaos and mayhem broke out within the cabinet. De Valera had been in Limerick the night the Treaty was signed and only heard of the conclusion from the late night newspapers. When he returned and called a meeting of his cabinet he made an immediate announcement that he would never support what had been concluded in London. He was incensed assuming that he would still have a majority within his seven man cabinet to overturn the outrageous Treaty. Stack and Brugha would side with de Valera without question making three certain to oppose the Treaty. The three cabinet members who had been in London, Griffith, Collins and Barton, would support their signature, thus only leaving W. T. Cosgrave to side with de Valera, as he thought. But Cosgrave was made of stronger stuff and insisted that the delegates be heard. And, most importantly, it was Cosgrave who reminded his colleagues that Griffith and his team had been sent as plenipotentiaries and not just as mere delegates. They therefore had the power to sign a Treaty. Cosgrave, having heard the arguments, sided with Griffith thus leaving those in favour in the majority. Piqued and shaken de Valera summoned the Dail to let every member have the chance to speak for or against what he considered a calamitous agreement.

And so was called perhaps the most important session of this embryonic parliament. The rowdy and ill-tempered meetings took place before and after Christmas. Collins made the thrust of his argument that the Treaty might not have given the Irish all that they wanted but it did give them the chance to make a beginning and declared that the Treaty was a springboard for the future of an independent Ireland. The fact that these crucial debates took place on either side of Christmas gave the country time to digest what had been reported to date. They wanted peace and they yearned for progress. In general they supported the Treaty. But would the Dail support it? The vote came on 7 January 1922 with 64 backing Griffith and just 57 agreeing with de Valera. Soon he resigned and left the Dail taking his adherents, including all six women members, with him. The die was cast. Agreement to push forward had won the day and Arthur Griffith was appointed as President with Michael Collins becoming Chairman of the Provisional Government. The British, for their part, acted swiftly passing the necessary legislation in the House of Commons and starting to evacuate their troops and administration from Dublin in double quick time. By the middle of January Dublin Castle had been handed over to Collins in an impressive ceremony at the castle.

The following six months, however, were to prove even more difficult for Collins than the previous years. To begin to administer a new state would take time, effort and a lot of patience. This was in short supply. The army of the new state proved troublesome since many of their leaders had been anti-Treaty. As the British vacated their barracks there was a mad scramble to take them over. Half went to those who supported the new government with the remainder falling into the hands of their opponents. By the spring of the year much of the south of the country, most of the province of Munster, was in the clutches of anti-Treaty personnel. They even seized a Royal Navy boat and stole a large quantity of weapons and ammunition. Much of Cork, Waterford and Kerry reverted to lawlessness and Collins told his colleagues that he considered the state of Ireland to be worse than it had been during the Black and Tan war.

In April the Four Courts building on the banks of the Liffey was captured by Rory O'Connor and anti-Treaty forces. They had brought their fight into the heart of the Irish capital; they had chosen this prestigious building to thumb their noses at Collins; they had thrown down the gauntlet to a frightened and terrified population. A General Election was to be held without further ado. This had been a requirement of the Treaty and the British were insisting that it be held immediately. Collins realised the urgency of the situation and even went so far as to enter into clandestine talks with de Valera to agree candidates for the election to represent their respective percentage positions. But this pact did not work out although the very fact that Collins had even talked to de Valera turned Griffith against him and these two become somewhat estranged at such a critical time for the country. The election was finally held on 16 June with a large majority of the people supporting the pro-Treaty side and, more importantly, peace for a troubled land. But Collins now had to listen to an irate Winston Churchill who demanded that the rebels be expelled from the Four Courts immediately. Griffith and Collins could only agree but were unsure how to oust O'Connor and his men from such an impregnable building. At length the British helped by lending some heavy artillery and men to fire upon the

Four Courts. The building fell and the insurgents flushed out and captured. Collins could, momentarily at least, breathe a sigh of relief but this only lasted a day or two. The Irish Civil War now erupted, the horror of horrors for the infant state.

The Irish Civil War

As the conflict quickly impacted upon the Free State, the destruction visited on the country during the War of Independence was once more repeated. The population only too abruptly realised that brother would be fighting against brother and father against son. The city of Dublin was devastated for the second time in just six years. In the first week Cathal Brugha, that dire opponent of Michael Collins, was killed in a hail of bullets during one of the early confrontations between the army and their anti-Treaty or 'irregular' enemies. Harry Boland, who had been Collins's close companion for so much of his life, was gunned down in a hotel in Skerries by a young inexperienced soldier. When Arthur Griffith, his co-founder of the Free State, died in hospital on 12 August, he was devastated and began to seriously consider his own mortality. He became the Commander-in-Chief of the Free State forces and, having donned his general's uniform, he immediately set out on a tour of visits to his men throughout the country. He seemed to have a premonition of disaster. One of his first visits was to his home county of Cork where he was not popular despite his attachments to that part of Ireland. Eamon de Valera was also in that area but they did not meet, although it was rumoured that Collins wanted to meet with his eminence grise to discuss a ceasefire.

The death of an Irish hero

Late on the evening of 22 August 1922, Collins was being driven, with an escort, through parts of west Cork he knew from his childhood. Shots rang out but, instead of quickly escaping the scene, General Collins insisted that his party stop and fight. Within a few minutes, Collins was hit in the head and died almost instantly. Much has been written about this deadly ambush at Beal na mBlath. Was he assassinated by a member of his own party? Was he killed by one of those who had been lying in wait for him? Had de Valera had a hand in the attack? These questions have never been satisfactorily answered. The fact of the matter was that Michael Collins was dead at the early age of 31. It took some time to transfer his body to a hospital in Cork and for it then to be taken for burial in Dublin by ship. The entire country was numbed by the early death of their hero, Michael Collins. He was buried at Glasnevin Cemetery with full military orders. And so, within the space of just ten days, the two founders of the modern day Free State were dead. The country was presented with yet another crisis of immense proportions. Into the gap precipitated by the deaths, W. T. Cosgrave and Kevin O'Higgins manfully stepped. Theirs would become a task of herculean magnitude. The question has often been asked. What if Collins had lived? It is, of course, impossible to accurately predict the answer. Collins certainly was the most charismatic of all the leading lights in Ireland at that time. He had a firm grasp on reality and had, what would have been so necessary, a clear understanding of economics and would have headed up an administration with a clear vision for the new Free State. He was an accomplished orator and had earned the respect of many world politicians, most of all the British. The quotation which will always be remembered was that uttered at the time of the signing of the Anglo-Irish Treaty – 'The Treaty gives us freedom, not the ultimate freedom that all nations desire and develop to, but the freedom to achieve it'. His loss was a tragedy of immense proportions for an Ireland which needed good fortune and not the colossal bad luck which it suffered on the death of Michael Collins.

Stings in the tail – other startling revelations in the life of a hero
Without going into a great deal of detail, but still worthy of mention, are a number of rather spectacular incidents relating to the life of this extraordinary man. The matters could well be left unsaid but,

to enthusiasts and aficionados of the Collins story, they need to be mentioned thus leaving no stone unturned and no dramatic episode of his life unrecorded. They may or may not dent the image of such an idol. Nonetheless, regardless of these revelations, Michael Collins did achieve much for the embryonic Irish Free State.

Michael Collins – the ladies' man

Collins was clearly attractive to, and attracted by, women during his short life. He was often described as a womaniser with a penchant for high society ladies. Having spent a fair amount of his political years in London, he had the opportunity to meet women like Hazel Lavery, Edith, Lady Londonderry and Moya Llewellyn Davies. Whether or not he did have affairs with any or all of them is a matter of conjecture although, on balance, there may well have been more than just an innocent romance between himself and Hazel Lavery. When he died she had to be dissuaded from wearing widow's weeds at his funeral. As far as Edith Londonderry is concerned there certainly was an affection between the lusty young man and the icon of London's fashionable titled dames. The story of Collins and Moya Llewellyn Davies, at least according to the author Vincent MacDowell, reveals even more startling titillation. They were rumoured not only to have had an affair but also two children, Richard and Kathleen, both of whom went on to great things in their own loves. Tantalisingly, however, little was said by either of them as to the rumour that they were the offspring of such a pimpernel as Michael Collins.

It should never be forgotten too, that both Collins and his friend, Harry Boland, were supposed to have been engaged at the same time to Kitty Kiernan from Granard. This was, of course, the most publicised romance between any woman and Michael Collins. Neither, sadly, lived to pursue their engagement to Kitty by being able to marry her.

Michael Collins – the homosexual

There were rumours too that Collins was a homosexual. The substance of this story most probably related to his method of letting off steam with his friends by 'having a bit of ear' and the enjoyment he so obviously evinced from this boisterous behaviour. The more rumours that abounded would lead people to believe that he must have had days that lasted 48 and not just 24 hours. The basic question would be – when did he ever have time to carry on all these activities and enter into such complex liaisons?

Michael Collins – his attitude to Northern Ireland

Collins hated what was going on in Northern Ireland; he despised the idea of his country being partitioned; he strove to bring Ireland together again. In the first months of partition he sent his fighters into the north to create havoc with the clear intention of bringing down its government. He saw the nationalist population being, in his eyes at any rate, subjected to pogroms, death and humiliation. He did what he could to retaliate with equal force and continue a war of attrition against the unionists. His action became so effective that, had it not been for the outbreak of the Civil War in the south and the removal of the IRA from the north, Northern Ireland could well have struggled to even survive. Events in the north were frightful and cruel and this was readily acknowledged by Prime Minister, James Craig. Collins met Craig on two occasions in an endeavour to rectify wrongs being perpetrated against the northern catholics, such as the expulsion of catholic workers from the Belfast shipyards. Craig showed courage even by meeting Collins at all but, although the two men did meet and actually liked one another, little of worth accrued from their deliberations. They had tried but, unfortunately, had only very limited success in their worthy endeavours.

Finally – Michael Collins – a man to remember

It must never be forgotten that Michael Collins was only seriously involved in Ireland's history for just six and a half years, from early

1916 on his return to Ireland from London, until his assassination in county Cork in August 1922. What he achieved in those few short years is nothing short of miraculous. To have been able to do so much he had to be totally ruthless and driven. This he certainly was. He will be remembered for his attention to detail; for his intolerance to bad time keeping and general sloppiness; for his ability to impress otherwise hard to impress people, like British politicians. Above all he will be lauded for his single mindedness for a free Ireland and peace for a country which he saw as having suffered centuries of ignominy and privation. His death was a blow to the whole of Ireland and his loss was felt not only by the Irish but by many other prominent peoples of the world.

Suggested reading

1. Coogan, Tim Pat, *Michael Collins – a Biography*, London, 1990.
2. Feehan, John M., *The Shooting of Michael Collins – Murder or Accident?*, Cork, 1981.
3. Hart, Peter, *Mick – the Real Michael Collins*, London, 2005.
4. MacDowell, Vincent, *Michael Collins and the Brotherhood*, Dublin, 1997.
5. Mackay, James, *Michael Collins – a Life*, Edinburgh, 1996.
6. O'Connor, Frank, *The Big Fellow – Michael Collins and the Irish Revolution*, Dublin, 1965.
7. Ryan, Meda, *The Day Michael Collins was Shot*, Dublin, 1989.
8. Stewart, A. T. Q., *Michael Collins – the Secret File*, Belfast, 1997.
9. Taylor, Rex, *Michael Collins*, London, 1958.

Kevin O'Higgins

Resolute and strong – an unbending
nation builder

Early life and a vocation

Kevin Christopher Higgins was born on 7 June 1892 in Stradbally, a little town in Queen's County, which today is county Laois. The family name at the time was Higgins, and it was Kevin who, as he approached adulthood, began to use the more Irish sounding surname O'Higgins. He was the fourth son, and fourth child of sixteen, born to Dr Thomas and Mrs Annie (nee Sullivan) and the family was a most respected one in the neighbourhood and county. Annie O'Higgins was the daughter of the equally well-known T.D. Sullivan who had been Lord Mayor of Dublin and previously an Irish Parliamentary MP.

Kevin loved being part of such a large family which soon moved out of the town to live at Woodlands, a farm on the outskirts of Stradbally. He always said that 'a man is only half a man if he has never lived or worked on a farm'. As a child he was particularly close to his younger sister, Kathleen, who later became a nun, and took pride in the fact that he acted as a barrier between his older brothers and his younger siblings to prevent them being unduly teased. But he was also intensely loyal to his older brothers.

His early schooling took place in the local convent in Stradbally and from there he progressed to the Christian Bothers in nearby Maryborough (today Port Laoise). He then made a further move, in his early teenage years, to the famous Jesuit College, Clongowes Wood, in county Kildare. There he made friends, some of whom would reappear in his later life. He was a first class pupil, excelling in classics and literature. And it was at this stage in his life that he became known as a practical joker and was forever performing tricks on friends and teachers alike. To those who know the story of Kevin O'Higgins this propensity to mischief of this kind seems almost anathema, but it is true and verifiable.

Then aged 15 Kevin made yet another move, this time to become a pupil at Knockbeg College in county Carlow. Here he was a star student, coming out best at classics and receiving high marks in English. And it was here at Knockbeg that he met a pretty young English teacher, Miss Brigid Cole, who would later become his wife. All in all Kevin O'Higgins had been an exemplary scholar and, aside from his practical joking, was considered by all his head teachers to have been one of their best and brightest pupils. His parents were pleased with their son's progress and now wondered in which direction his life would proceed. They were to be surprised and really rather shocked.

Kevin professed a priestly vocation, much to everyone's astonishment. Few, if any, of those around him realised his desire to pursue Holy Orders but it was not long before he was accepted as a student at Maynooth College. His studies commenced well enough but soon he started to deviate from his chosen vocation. Rather than following the good example of those around him, Kevin rebelled. He was a smoker and the habit was strictly forbidden at the college. This had been a diktat of the late Cardinal Logue and a rule not to be broken. Students contravening this directive were given three chances and if the offending student was caught for the third time, he was automatically expelled. Kevin was a bright student with a number of tolerant and helpful teachers, one of whom was able to assist him. He was duly expelled after his third offence but was given the chance, through the good offices of his English professor, to continue his vocation at a seminary in county Carlow. But there he played too many practical jokes and sailed too close to the wind and soon fell from grace. He was dismissed from this college as well. He felt now that he could no longer pursue his calling and gave up the idea of his ever becoming a priest.

Examining his options, Kevin decided to enter University College in Dublin to study arts and the law. But the Kevin O'Higgins of old, the fun loving practical joker and bon viveur, had lost his zest for life. He became taciturn, jaded and gloomy. His friends did not recognise him. He found himself totally bored and the prospect of a career in the law seemed unattractive and unappealing. He took to drink and was only able to survive financially by writing articles for the Dublin newspapers. Events in Ireland then took a hand in shaping the career of this enigma of a young man. His life would now change, and change forever.

The Volunteers, the First World War and the Easter Rising

After the Irish Volunteers were formed towards the end of 1913, mainly in response to the Ulster Volunteers who had organised earlier in the year, Kevin took time to think over whether he would join or not. He harboured doubts about the organisation but, at length, in the autumn of 1914, after the start of the Great War, he did sign up. There was, in his own family household, a difference of opinion about that other matter, to join up to fight the Germans or to stay at home and fight for Ireland. For some of his brothers it was simple. They joined up to fight in Europe and, in fact, one of Kevin's brothers, Michael, died in the war. But, like his father, Kevin held to the Irish nationalist view and did not.

Kevin was present at the graveside of Jeremiah O'Donovan Rossa, the old Fenian who had died in America and whose body had been returned to Dublin for a martyr's burial. And it was here that Kevin became aware of Patrick Pearse, whose name would soon become immortalised in Irish history. Pearse delivered the oration that day in August 1915 which included the words 'but the fools, the fools, the fools; they have left us our Fenian dead, and while Ireland holds these graves, Ireland unfree shall never be at peace'. Kevin had no doubt that his decision to join the Volunteers was the right one. His heart had quickened, like those of so many others, at Pearse's words and he was ready to follow the lead set by Pearse and his friends.

When the Easter Rising broke out in late April 1916, Kevin O'Higgins was ready to fight. But, like all young men trying to reach Dublin to join the rebels, he was prevented from entering the city. In fact he got no further than Athy in county Kildare, some forty miles from the city. He had to sit it out back at home realising that they could never beat the British militarily but knowing that the Rising had captured the imagination of the world taking place, as it did of course, in the middle of the world war.

He now returned to study, this time at Cork University where he read law. There he played a prominent part in student politics, his appetite for action all the more aroused following the Rising. By 1917 he was in the thick of organising the Volunteers in Queen's County. He was the captain of the Stradbally Volunteers and, although his was not an onerous task, he did his job conscientiously by opposing vigorously the threat of conscription during 1918.

Kevin O'Higgins was, by now, making a name for himself in politics. Before the war was over he stood at the Offaly by-election where his speeches from the platform were considered brilliant by his supporters and as treasonous by the authorities. He was arrested and in court he vigorously defended himself by challenging the statements made by the police. His self-defence, however, was to no avail and he was sentenced to five months in jail. He served the complete tariff by refusing to be of good behaviour. A part of his sentence was spent at Crumlin Road prison in Belfast.

Upon his release as the war was ending he stood for Sinn Fein (a name given to the opponents of the Irish Parliamentary Party) for his home county of Queen's County (Laois). He was elected along with another 72 from his party, none of whom, as their manifesto had declared, would be taking their seats at Westminster. These new MPs (or TDs as they came to be called) met on 21 January 1919 in the new local (and of course still illegal) parliament, the Dail, and O'Higgins was chosen as W. T. Cosgrave's assistant at the Ministry of Local Government. He had, almost incidentally, just passed his LLB exams with First Class honours. But his first priority was to serve Dail Eireann and the new Ireland as he saw it.

As he worked in his new role, there were the great difficulties of the British authorities trying to capture ministers and disrupt their local administration. Despite the problems of moving from place to place to avoid arrest and being permanently 'on the run', O'Higgins and his colleagues carried out a remarkably good job in most trying circumstances. Their work may have been clandestine but they were able to improve the lot of many ordinary Irish people, something the British had failed to do. As time went on secret courts and tribunals met and delivered judgements which were admired even by the members of the ascendancy who, from time to time, appeared at the Sinn Fein courts seeking justice, and getting it. Kevin O'Higgins revelled in his position. It seemed to suit his personality and as he regularly escaped the clutches of the Royal Irish Constabulary, the more the adrenalin rush assisted him in carrying out the duties allotted to him. To add to his responsibilities he decided to assist in the collection of the National Loan which had been instigated by Michael Collins. Needless to say this was another immense risk for him and would be yet another excuse for the British to arrest him. But he diligently stuck to his task and carried on with his busy schedule. In such a small county as Queen's County, his chances of capture were even more likely but he was not to be put off and did his duty. He had come to greatly admire Collins who, in many ways was like himself, a man to tolerate no slacking from the work in hand.

Kevin was soon in the horns of another dilemma. Because of his Roman Catholic faith and beliefs he knew it was an excommunicable offence to join an oath bound society. But at this time many Irish men and women were becoming members of the Irish Republican Brotherhood (IRB) and he was drawn to sign up. This he did, after some heart searching, during 1920 but it was not long until his conscience got the better of him and he soon resigned. Another prominent figure of the time, Eamon de Valera, was in a similar quandary and did not join either.

He was fortunate to have appointed as his secretary Rory O'Connor, a determined young man suited to the jobs O'Higgins had for him to undertake. O'Connor was to feature later in the life of Kevin O'Higgins. As his job became more and more stressful O'Higgins's popularity sunk. He did not endear himself to many with whom he came in contact and started to write offensive letters.

This suited his boss, W. T. Cosgrave, for he simply got O'Higgins to send off hard hitting letters, a job he was not keen to do himself. And it was also a novel way of diverting O'Higgins' aggression on to someone else. Cosgrave had, for too long, been the brunt of the younger man's displeasure. However we should not be distracted from the fact that Kevin O'Higgins was an accomplished administrator who revelled in the job he had been given.

The war of independence and the Treaty talks

Throughout the duration of this Anglo-Irish conflict, O'Higgins continued to be a marked man 'on the run'. He managed to avoid capture on a number of occasions and his use of aliases such as 'Mr Casey' and 'Mr Wilson' helped him to keep out of harm's way. His brother, Brian, still a schoolboy but very active in the war, was seized as was Dr O'Higgins, his father. Both were roughly treated during their incarceration at the Curragh and subsequently at Mountjoy prison in Dublin.

In the midst of the struggle, the Dail continued to meet and function as best it could. O'Higgins was often invited by de Valera to attend his cabinet meetings although he was not a member of the executive. This pleased Kevin who revered, though did not always agree with, his chief; he greatly respected Arthur Griffith but found him a bad judge of men and he considered Austin Stack and Cathal Brugha to be incompetent and lacking in vision.

De Valera had gone to London in the summer of 1921 to negotiate Ireland's future with David Lloyd George. The outcome was unsatisfactory and, back in Dublin, the executive pondered on what to do next. In October a team led by Griffith and Collins but not, significantly, accompanied by de Valera, returned to the lion's den at 10 Downing Street. The team needed secretaries and O'Higgins was asked to go in this capacity. But he declined the offer as he was about to be married to Brigid Cole, his former English teacher at Knockbeg College. The wedding took place in the October at the same time as the Treaty talks. Rory O'Connor was Kevin's best man and Eamon de Valera attended as a guest. Michael Collins sent a gift for the young couple and tickets for a theatre show. This was a typical kindness always shown by Collins whose life continued to be a frenetic one.

On reflecting about the talks, Kevin always considered that it had been a detrimental move to send Erskine Childers as a secretary. Although greatly liked by de Valera, he was despised, and even as much as hated, by Arthur Griffith. O'Higgins' presence was missed in London on the secretarial staff. He also thought that de Valera should have led the Irish delegation himself and told him so in no uncertain terms. When, on 6 December 1921, the Irish signed the Treaty, the reaction in Dublin was devastating. O'Higgins felt that de Valera should have backed his men who had been, after all, sent as plenipotentiaries. Initially he himself did not like the Treaty but had enough sense to reconsider and give it his support. Like he always did, Kevin O'Higgins appreciated that the country needed to be united and he fought to help establish this position.

But de Valera and his right hand men in Dublin, Stack and Brugha, voted against the acceptance of the terms agreed by Griffith and his team. Had it not been for the seventh member of the executive, W. T. Cosgrave, who agreed with negotiators, the vote would have gone the other way. Kevin saw the split in the cabinet as unforgivable but not, he admitted, entirely surprising. Debates on the Treaty were held and, for many days on both sides of Christmas, the speeches ranged from most supportive to downright antagonistic. As a TD himself, O'Higgins made a long, mature and statesmanlike contribution. What he said was clear and concise; it was pointed and direct and it put him firmly on the side of acceptance. Many commended his speech and his imperious style singled him out for greatness. When, in the end, the Treaty was agreed by 64 votes to 57 and Arthur Griffith chosen to replace the petulant de Valera as President, it was time to move on.

Griffith chose O'Higgins as his Minister of Economic Affairs in his provisional government. The British had already started to move out of Dublin leaving the way open for the Irish to run their own affairs. The first six months of 1922 were, however, a most chaotic time with the 'irregulars' (those who had voted against the Treaty) creating mayhem with murders, burnings and disruption of every kind. Included in the number of anti-Treatyites was Rory O'Connor, Kevin's best man and good friend. The closeness between these men was soon severed. A General Election was also due to allow the people their say but was postponed until June when matters crucially came to a head.

There were continuing talks being held in London and O'Higgins attended as an aide to Collins. He made an excellent negotiator and was renowned for his straight talking and his 'no nonsense' attitude, always allowing his opponent to speak for as long as he liked and then taking his chance to counter what had been said. It was also around this time that he became aware of the vivacious and alluring Hazel Lavery, the wife of the famous painter, Sir John Lavery.

The election and the civil war

The General Election was eventually held in mid June although the much-publicised constitution was only published the day before. The people had therefore no chance whatsoever to consider the proposals for the future of the Free State. The British had been pressing Collins and Griffith to proceed, without any more delay, to hold the election. Collins, realising how difficult this would be, secretly came up with a compromise on the issue of candidates with de Valera. O'Higgins appreciated the urgency for the country to go to the polls and acquiesced with the furtive arrangement whereby candidates representing the pro- and anti-Treaty sides would proportionately be permitted to stand for the Dail. Independents would also be allowed to stand. The outcome was straightforward. The people voted three to one for peace and voted in Collins, Griffith and their colleagues as well as many of the Labour and Independent candidates. The compromise had backfired on de Valera but this proved to be the least of the Free State's concerns. The anti-Treatyites, led by Rory O'Connor, who had captured the Four Courts, were ordered out of their lair and, although given a deadline to surrender, they refused to budge. With the assistance of British soldiers and their weaponry, the rebels were blasted out and forced to surrender. The Irish Civil War had erupted with a vengeance.

Scarcely had the war begun and the anti-Treaty rebels expelled from Dublin, the tragedy starkly epitomised by the death of Cathal Brugha in a hail of bullets in the city centre, than Collins and O'Higgins joined the military. Michael Collins became the Commander-in-Chief and immediately started to move around the country supporting and encouraging his forces. Progress was being made and their enemies were being driven from their hideouts and incarcerated.

Tragically then the infant state suffered the loss of its two courageous leaders within the space of just ten days. Arthur Griffith, that gallant stalwart of Ireland's rebirth, died in hospital on 12 August. He had been unwell but had continued on with his stressful job. On 22 August in county Cork not far from his birthplace, Michael Collins was assassinated. Kevin O'Higgins was badly affected by the news. Normally a stoical and measured young man, he broke down in tears in the presence of his wife. The country was inconsolable and even the enemies of the state were fulsome in their praise of the two lost men. The Free State had experienced the most tragic start imaginable but, although in the midst of a struggle for its very existence, it had to keep going. Kevin O'Higgins was soon to prove his mettle and Kevin O'Higgins it was who steadied the embryonic Free State ship and kept it afloat.

W. T. Cosgrave took the helm. Although not everyone's first choice and not, for that matter O'Higgins' who would initially have preferred Patrick Hogan, those appointed to the cabinet quickly got in behind the new leader to face the tremendous challenges ahead. O'Higgins was chosen as Minister of Home Affairs and, in effect, Cosgrave's deputy. He was just 30 years old yet he faced his task with fortitude and resolve. Such was the chaotic state of the country that all the ministers and their wives had to live in government buildings under guard. It was clearly too dangerous to be living at their own homes. Thus Brigid O'Higgins soon joined her husband to live out the next months in a state of unreality, but at least safe unreality.

The government got on with its business soon deciding to assimilate the former Dail with the provisional government. They steered through the constitution although with considerable difficulty and opposition. O'Higgins was the chief architect in persuading the TDs on every side to accept the need to pass this vital bill to get on with daily business. Kevin O'Higgins was the strong man of the parliament and acknowledged as such by the majority of those within as well as those without the Dail.

The iron fist

With disruption still holding sway in many parts of the country and with the problems of keeping the military loyal to the government, the time had come to ensure that law and order, of recent times almost broken down, would prevail. The two leaders, Cosgrave and O'Higgins, were of one mind. Nothing but the introduction of an iron fist would suffice to win the hearts and minds of a bewildered populace. It was at this time that O'Higgins' clarity of thought and rigid determination became evident. What would happen over the succeeding months would shock and offend many people but those who really understood the critical state that Ireland was in would not baulk at the harsh and ruthless powers soon to be enacted.

The military were given extensive and punitive powers, including the ultimate sanction of the death penalty. Those found in possession of firearms or explosives would be summarily executed. Clearly O'Higgins was seen as the instigator of this far-reaching and ruthless legislation. In the Dail there were countless vociferous speeches against these enactments but all from opposition TDs who did not have to rule and keep peace in the country. It was not a happy time for the democrat but the cabinet kept the line and supported the iron-willed O'Higgins who sincerely believed that all government is based on force and that it must meet force with greater force if it is to survive.

On 17 November 1922 the first executions took place. Four young men, arrested in possession of arms, were put to death, the first of what was to be 77 executions during this period. However the chief bête noire and thorn in the flesh of the government, Erskine Childers, by now a hated opponent of O'Higgins, was sentenced to death for possessing a small pistol given to him as a gift by Michael Collins. His defence held no water and Childers faced a firing squad with calm and serenity on 24 November. Kevin O'Higgins, the strong man of the government now attracted to himself the hatred of the republicans. It seemed the writing was on the wall for the minister who had driven through such powerful and reviled legislation. But he did forcibly declare, in regard to Childers' execution, that it would be unfair to execute the friendless and spare the influential. With these pointed words, the government moved on.

Ministers were now threatened with assassination but carried on regardless. The situation then took a fearful turn for the worse on 7 December when two TDs, Sean Hales and Padraic O'Maille, were shot in Dublin city centre. Hales died and O'Maille was badly injured but their assailants were never captured. The immediate outcome was to rock Dublin and the Free State even more starkly than had the execution of Erskine Childers. The cabinet met at once and decided unanimously to put to death four republican prisoners, one representing each of Ireland's provinces. Those wakened from the sleep and brought to their place of execution were Liam Mellowes, Richard Barrett, Joseph McKelvey and Rory O'Connor. Many saw this as an act of reprisal but, on reflection, more a case of a decision 'pour encourager les autres'. It seemed to have the desired effect for no further TDs were ever attacked for the duration of the Civil War although the republicans continued to burn the homes of senators and other businesses whose staff and owners supported the government. It goes without saying that O'Connor's death remained to haunt O'Higgins for the rest of his life.

Kevin O'Higgins had no time to rest. His next assignment was to reorganise the police. The RIC was disbanded, although the Dublin Metropolitan Police were, for the time being, retained. The forming of a police force was essential for the new regime. It was, of course, O'Higgins who prepared the way for the Garda Siochana and it was on his insistence that it was to be an unarmed force. In such difficult circumstances, the guards performed their duties well and were assisted by a reformed judiciary and court system. But as he proceeded to introduce these further measures to settle the Free State, those opposed to him, mainly the republican element, were determined to threaten and intimidate him. He was unmoved and it was this enduring doggedness and strength of will which drove him on. It was to be his lasting epitaph.

But sadly the sword of Damocles was soon to fall upon young O'Higgins and his family. On 23 February 1923 his family home at Stradbally was entered by a group of armed irregulars and, after a struggle, his father, Dr Thomas Higgins, was shot dead. When he heard the tragic news O'Higgins broke down but, typical of the man, he declared that this heinous crime would not deflect him from his task of building up the new state. By now he was styled vice President of the Dail and along with the President, W. T. Cosgrave, he clearly saw what had to be done and was resolute in pursuing his goal.

The end of the Civil War and trouble with the army

Various futile attempts were made throughout the last months of 1923 and the early ones of 1924 to bring the destructive civil struggle to an end. The weary citizens of the Free State wanted an end to warfare to enable them to savour peace throughout their new state. But this goal was a difficult one to achieve. With many more Irishmen being executed for possession of arms peace seemed as far away as ever. The commander of the irregulars, Liam Lynch, was killed in the Knockmealdown mountains in county Tipperary on 10 April 1923 thus hastening the end for the determined and callous guerrilla fighters. Eamon de Valera, hitherto an unimportant, yet a political, soldier tried to assert some authority and come to some compromise with the government. Attempts were made to broker a ceasefire and, had it not been for O'Higgins' utter determination, such an arrangement might have been concluded. Kevin O'Higgins would not agree to any demands of the irregulars and, although often a difficult task, he usually managed to bring his cabinet colleagues with him. He declared that 'this is not going to be a draw with a replay in the autumn'. He stuck to his guns and emphasised his strength of mind by severely punishing crime and even using flogging as a deterrent. He was, in many quarters, universally hated for his iron fist tactics but he would not change his view regardless of the obvious danger it brought to his own life.

A truce of sorts was eventually agreed upon in May 1924 when the irregulars laid down their arms. Many of these weapons were hidden away and not surrendered to the army but at least the killings were over. The cost to the infant Irish economy was huge although the British government did agree to help to bail out the Free State's finances. During the War of Independence and the Civil War, millions of pounds worth of property and businesses had been destroyed; many of the fine old ascendancy houses had been razed to the ground in spiteful acts of vengeance; many innocent civilians and soldiers of the state, as well as those opposed to it, had been murdered and cut down in their prime. It was a time of shame for the country and it was clear that only a firm hand would return it to any semblance of normality. And the man who was left to achieve this near impossibility was Kevin O'Higgins.

As the Dail introduced more and more pieces of necessary legislation, the more many baulked at it. O'Higgins and Cosgrave pushed through what was essential to steady the ship of state. More troubles were, however, in store. There had never been any love lost between O'Higgins and Richard Mulcahy, the Commander-in-Chief of the army who had succeeded the late lamented Michael Collins. Cabinet meetings were fraught with arguments and dissension concerning the role of the army and its adherence to their political masters. By March 1924 Mulcahy had resigned and not long afterwards the army generals were sacked. This act, though taken and agreed by the entire cabinet, was seen as a further example of vindictiveness by O'Higgins. This drew more opprobrium upon him and his rigid stance made him enemies on both sides of the army, both those opposed to and those who supported the government. In retrospect O'Higgins had done the right thing; he had done well in keeping the newly emerging country on an even keel. But the writing was on the wall. He had made too many enemies, he was too unpopular and he had too few friends.

Kevin O'Higgins – the man

Those who knew O'Higgins in his youth realised that he was destined for greatness. Many may not have liked him but they recognised his phenomenal potential. After the problems and difficulties of the past months O'Higgins, rather than easing off, pushed forward relentlessly. For some time Cosgrave had been unwell and forbidden by his doctors to attend meetings of the Dail since they were so stressful and injurious to his health. Needless to say O'Higgins stood up to the mark and took control. But he remained unpopular. An example of this dislike was when he laid a wreath at the Cenotaph in London during the Remembrance Day ceremonies after Cosgrave had declined to attend. But, as ever, O'Higgins knew he had done the right thing and refused to bow to public pressure. He then introduced legislation against the liquor trade by curtailing the opening hours of public houses. This action was regarded as a detestable act by O'Higgins, by now the Minister of Justice.

As a committed Roman Catholic Kevin O'Higgins could certainly never have been described as a bigot. He was scrupulously fair in dealings with any Irish man or woman, regardless of their religious conviction. As a devoted parent, he cherished the time, short as it often was, with his wife and daughter, Maeve. In November 1924 Brigid and Kevin lost their little son at only twelve days old. He was devastated but, as ever, he got on with his work. His second daughter, Una, was born in January 1927.

O'Higgins, in summary, was a clear thinker and a Triton amongst minnows. He was a man, a politician, ahead of his time. Realising his reputation he often had a premonition of an early death, even by assassination. Within a few short months his intuition proved, sadly and unfortunately, only too accurate.

Representations for the state

Thrust as he was into the limelight, representation at the 1925 Disarmament Conference was an important role for O'Higgins. He also attended Commonwealth conferences and he usually made good use of his contacts from other countries. He became a firm supporter of the way Canada approached membership of the British Commonwealth and the Canadians reciprocated, finding O'Higgins the type of man they could work with. For such a young man, he was proving to be a more than useful asset to the Free State and one prepared to challenge decisions made by Britain. Generally he was liked and even King George V was charmed by O'Higgins's performance. In 1926 he represented the Free State once more by his attendance at the League of Nations gathering in Geneva.

Relations with the new state of Northern Ireland were at all times uppermost in the mind of the TDs in the Free State parliament. O'Higgins, as ever, was to the fore in the discussions with the northern politicians. To begin with he was wary of the unionists but he found Sir James Craig much more reasonable than he had predicted and in fact he proved amenable and helpful. There were two major issues concerning Northern Ireland, the Boundary Commission and finance.

The members of the Dail were anxious to hear the conclusions of the commission on the border for they assumed, wrongly as it was to turn out, that large parts of Northern Ireland, particularly counties Tyrone and Fermanagh and perhaps south Down, would be returned to the Free State. But as the months and years went by the commission continued to delay the publication of their recommendations. In the end, after the resignation of Eoin MacNeill, the chairman, it was decided to let the border remain as it had been at the time of partition. This fudge outraged many but O'Higgins, in his usual clinical method of thinking, considered that it was time to move on. On finances there were debates with Westminster politicians regarding who owed what to whom. Once more there was vociferous, but vacuous, comment amongst the Irish and an agreement of sorts was brokered. In effect the Free State came out of the negotiations relatively well and O'Higgins was satisfied.

Hardly a day passed or a debate in the Dail concluded than the partition question was not brought up. O'Higgins, though intrinsically a nationalist and a separatist, had his own views on this interminable dispute. He recalled the position taken by Arthur Griffith in which he had supported a dual monarchy for Ireland. He sincerely felt that the British monarch could also be the monarch of Ireland. He believed that unionists would acquiesce to become part of a united country which had the king or queen as head of state. The nationalists would also agree that, as long as Ireland had its independence, then it would be acceptable to have a titular monarch in charge. This idea may today seem far-fetched, and understandably so, but in the mid 1920s such a solution was readily attainable and acceptable. The more Kevin O'Higgins thought of this possible outcome, the more he liked it. He even foresaw the king being crowned in Phoenix Park by the two archbishops. Perhaps this was a step too far but he did think it a distinct possibility given a fair wind.

When he was attending various London conferences he was making friends with many British politicians. They were beginning to like O'Higgins and accept many of what they saw as his rational arguments on various previously contentious issues. Under his leadership the Irish delegation made great strides, something appreciated in London, but not universally so in Dublin. Debates in the Dail often turned into slanging matches but O'Higgins took these attacks on his integrity calmly and without rancour.

The end came quickly – if not unexpectedly

During 1927 a General Election took place. O'Higgins and Cosgrave were weary as were the ministers in their cabinet. Theirs had been an onerous and often unequal task as they struggled with the duties of state. O'Higgins, determined not to stand again in his home county of Laois following the killing of his father, stood in south Dublin. There in a seat with a high proportion of unionist voters he won easily but the result was disappointing for his party. They lost seats and ended up with just 47 TDs. De Valera's group, which still refused to enter the Dail on account of the oath, retained their 44 seats. The government of Cosgrave, of course, continued in power but the writing was on the wall. De Valera would soon bring his new Fianna Fail party into parliament and he would take control in 1932.

The brutal end came on Sunday 10 July 1927. As he emerged from church at Booterstown after midday mass, Kevin O'Higgins was gunned down by a number of assassins. He lay dying in the street and was brought home where five hours later he died from his wounds. Never were the killers brought to justice but with his dying breath, O'Higgins forgave those who had attacked him. His prediction of his early death had come true. The man who truly shaped the Free State in the early years of its existence had been taken from a country so much in need of his clear sightedness. Long would the Free State mourn his passing.

Kevin O'Higgins's state funeral a few days later was a grand and solemn affair. Those who followed his coffin dressed in their morning suits and top hats had time to reflect what might have been. Many would have mourned him as a dear and devoted friend and companion, like his wife, his little daughters, his extended family and his closest friend, Patrick Hogan, who had lived in the O'Higgins household. Others would have been his strongest opponents who might perhaps have regretted their verbal attacks on O'Higgins during his lifetime. But all realised that a very special man had gone from their midst. It is surely time, even in the early days of the twenty first century and over eighty years since his death, to bring the name and ideas and visions of Kevin O'Higgins back into focus when considering the stage Ireland has reached today.

A curious addendum to the life of Kevin O'Higgins

The story of the life of Kevin O'Higgins is, however, incomplete. This serious and hard working man had another, more secretive, side to his intensely busy life; this almost religious zealot with the cold persona did possess a stunningly contrasting alter ego. Not long after his marriage to Brigid Cole, he fell in love, and in fact became besotted with, Hazel Lavery, the London socialite and wife of the Belfast born painter, Sir John Lavery. She had herself been deeply in love with Michael Collins and with whom she had an intense relationship (although denied by many) and who had been inconsolable when he was murdered in county Cork in August 1922.

O'Higgins had met Hazel during his frequent visits to London when he was representing the new Free State government at meetings with British ministers and attending various conferences with other Commonwealth countries. Hazel Lavery, being the consummate hostess and fashion icon, had the knack of bringing together all the leading politicians and their wives to her stylish home at Cromwell Place. She was the kind of person who could melt the hearts of powerful men, not only with her good looks but also with her ability for making introductions. She was regularly able to assist the inexperienced Irish politicians meet their influential

British counterparts. And it was in such a circumstance that Kevin O'Higgins was to meet his paramour.

The couple began to meet often and furtively although many knew that there was more than met the eye in this relationship. O'Higgins wrote incessantly to Hazel and even started to send her love poems. He was infatuated with her and in one of his letters he declared to Hazel that 'you are my life and my breath, my sun and air and wind'. Sir John Lavery, who had to turn many a blind eye to his wife's romantic attachments, decided to take Hazel to America to accompany him whilst he carried out lots of painting commissions. This was his way of firmly, but gently, separating O'Higgins from his wife. Twice in a period of eighteen months Hazel was required to accompany her husband to America, much to her displeasure. During these enforced separations, Hazel and Kevin corresponded and Hazel was always looking forward to her return to London to meet Kevin again. Meetings between the pair also took place in Dublin from time to time at such places as the Royal Dublin Horse Show and at the Vice Regal Lodge where the Governor General, Tim Healy, a friend of the Laverys, often entertained. When O'Higgins himself was assassinated in July 1927, Hazel was every bit as devastated as she had been following Collins' death in August 1922. She 'wallowed in grief and self accusation' and could not be consoled.

The question could now be asked – what about O'Higgins' relations with his wife and family? Hazel Lavery's biographer, Sinead O'Coole, writing in the late 1990s, is certain that there was an estrangement and even a separation between Kevin and his wife, Brigid. No mention is made of any love affair by O'Higgins's 1948 biographer, Terence de Vere White. This may have been on account of his sense of propriety and decorum in those more refined days after World War Two. Neither is it for me to judge the O'Higgins/Hazel Lavery relationship but it does seem strange that such a significant part of O'Higgins's life, especially during those most critical days for the new Free State in the mid 1920s, is not even mentioned in White's book.

Suggested reading
1. McCarthy, John P., *Kevin O'Higgins – Builder of the Irish State*, Dublin, 2006.
2. White, Terence de Vere, *Kevin O'Higgins*, Dublin, 1986 (latest edition)